MW01289671

The Real Before The Estate

What I Wish I Knew Before I Started Real Estate

Chastin J. Miles

Copyright

Before You Read

This book was written based on my knowledge and past experiences. References or income examples of my business and/or the examples of others are not guaranteed. Your success is dependent on your application of the information presented. I highly recommend that you seek the assistance of a licensed real estate and/or mortgage professional before making your final decisions. All names and personas have been replaced with character names for privacy purposes.

CONTENTS

CONTENTS

CONTENTS

PART 5: UNDERSTANDING THE BUSINESS

PART 6: WORKING THE BUSINESS

CONTENTS

Introduction

Embarking on a new journey will make you feel two ways. On one hand, you will feel excited; but on the other hand, you will feel nervous as crap. The excitement comes from knowing that you are about to do something new. You are ready to take charge and potentially do something great for yourself. The nervousness comes in when you think about what could happen if it doesn't work out. Our biggest fear as entrepreneurs is FAILURE. The thought of failing can make any savvy entrepreneur think twice when it comes to making a life-changing business decision. I don't know anyone who starts a business expecting to fail, but I do know people who start businesses and end up failing. There are many factors that could increase failure. We can blame the economy, our team, or even our childhood. On the opposite hand, when we reach success, we typically don't blame anyone but ourselves. It's so interesting, but it's so true. The thought of failing has prevented many people from doing really great things. I've personally tried to encourage many of my closest friends to start businesses around their talents. In my head, I knew if they would make their talents available to the world, they would be wildly successful. They just didn't know it for themselves. I would have conversations with them just to have many of them compare themselves to me. They would say, "*I can't, or I'm not you, or what if it doesn't work?*" It was discouraging to hear. I would try my hardest say to them the complete opposite, but I've learned that you can't force people to be great, especially adults. People are going to do what they want to do. If they fail or if they succeed, it's on them. This concept is the same for real estate agents. Think for a moment into the future. Your future as a real estate agent.

When you look forward 5 years from now, would you attach the word success or failure to yourself? I would imagine you would see yourself as successful. With that thought in mind, I'm here to tell you, it will all based around the actions you take now and in the near future.

Thanks to social media and reality TV, the lifestyle of a real estate agent is now something people all across the world strive to have. The real estate business opportunity is one of the greatest opportunities in history. Who wouldn't want to become a real estate agent? Unfortunately, I would also go as far as to say that it's one of the most glamorized careers today. Being a real estate agent is almost like being a celebrity. As a matter of fact, us agents have to market ourselves as if we are celebrities just to get our names and faces in front of people. You've probably come across some agent headshots that look like they belong in a high-end fashion magazine. It's the new way of marketing ourselves. What does this say about actually getting the job done though?

The cool thing about becoming a real estate agent is that it will give you the ability to not only help families with homes, but also to make a lot of money doing it. We all love money, right? Being in a position where you can make a ton of money with the ability to create long lasting wealth for yourself is the best position ever.

When I decided to become a real estate agent, I had no clue what I was getting myself into. I'm not saying that in a bad way or anything; I'm simply saying that there were so many surprises ahead of me and I had no earthly clue that they were coming.

Growing up, I always knew I wanted to be an entrepreneur. I wanted to be one before I could even spell it. At that time, the only reason I wanted to become an entrepreneur was because I didn't want to work for anyone else. I know that sounds crazy to some people. Who do I think I am, right? Your thoughts would have been right in line with mine. I even didn't know who I was. I just knew that I wanted to create my own path, whatever that looked like.

Growing up, I wanted to be anything and everything. I wanted to be an artist. I wanted to be a performer. I wanted to be a lawyer. I wanted to be a lot of things. The funny thing is, I felt like I could do them all, too. I didn't feel like I ever wanted to limit my focus on one thing. What's even funnier is, that isn't how I was raised. I was told to graduate high school, go to college, get a job, and retire. The good ole American way. Clearly, I chose to go a different route.

As the career path of an entrepreneur, in this case a real estate agent, becomes more and more glamorous, being a business owner gets easier and easier. The work doesn't get easier, but the access gets easier. Access to resources like this book and videos and trainings. All of this to help you along the way.

When I got into the business, I had one mission. That mission was to make money. I knew there was huge earning potential in the real estate business. Anytime I heard the words— real estate, it was a conversation about a lot of money. In high school, I had friends whose parents were real estate brokers, and guess what, they had a lot of money. Growing up, money was something my family and I didn't have a lot of. Actually, we barely had any. I didn't even know basic fundamentals when it came to money, and I don't think my parents did either. I didn't know what was a lot verses what was barely getting by. We were just living. My mother worked extremely hard to support us, and she did what she could. Because of that, I knew that I needed money to be able to at least do what she did. I didn't know exactly what I wanted to buy with money, but as I got older, I got ideas. Thats where it all started. An idea was all I needed to give me that little push to create something better for myself and my family.

As you get into this book, you'll read about the challenges I've faced along this path I've been on. But, this isn't an autobiography or anything. I simply want to make sure you know the things I had to go through to get to where I am today. By no means did any of my successes fall from the sky into my lap. It was all a series of the right...and wrong steps. In an effort to make sure you keep reading, I'm not going to talk about how hard things were for me, at this point in the book. That's not the impression I want to give this early in your mission. The lesson I want you to get right now is that *anything is possible*. If that sounds a bit cliché, it's because it is. All successful people say, "*anything is possible*." Some of my mentors even add on the words, "*if you work hard*." True story though, I didn't really believe that until I experienced it for myself. To me, that was dreamer talk. Being in the game for the time I have been, I now know that the possibilities are endless and that I shouldn't feel like I can't do something. When you reach a certain level, even if it's not the top, you begin to get a different perspective on how things work and what's actually attainable. Things that may have seemed out of reach, or even impossible before, now seem like they are right in front of you.

As I began to make business moves, I also grew in many areas of my life. As you will read, I was barely into adulthood when I chose to go down this path. I was far from maturity in many areas. I've even tried to retrace my steps to see what I did to get certain places, and even thats been more difficult than it sounds. I have grown in many areas. I've gained a new sense of patience. I've reached new levels of understanding. Even my faith has gotten stronger. The possible biggest areas of growth for me has been my persistence. Being persistent in my day to day actions takes me to new levels everyday. You name it, I've probably grown from it. The best part about this is, there are more lessons that I know are right in front of me, and I'm ready for them. It makes me excited to even think about it.

I've tried so many things in my real estate business, hoping that they would give me the big break I was looking for. I was always looking for that feeling of instant gratification. I would try something and end up failing at it, then move on. Then I would fail again, and again, and again. I didn't have any persistence behind my actions. What I noticed though is, out of every one of those failures, there was a lesson. It was during the times of failure that I would learn these lessons and experience the real growth. Each and every time, there was something I learned that actually propelled me. I didn't see it at that moment because of my immaturity, but I see it now. The growth that I've experienced in my business actually came from moments of failure. A big listing I landed came from failing at the 5 previous listing appointments before it. The buyer I finally got to trust me to help them buy a house, came as a result of being rejected by the 20 previous buyer leads. The failure and rejection was exactly what I needed to really make this work. This is so important because every time I failed, I WANTED to give up. Sometimes I actually gave up what I was doing at that moment. I remember the time I was ready to throw in the towel because I was convinced that real estate just wasn't for me. Clearly I didn't or you wouldn't be reading this but this was just another sign of my immature thinking. Luckily, my thinking didn't get the best of me. In all the failure, I kept telling myself one thing. I CAN'T QUIT...EVER.

When you're reading this book, you'll notice that I get straight to the point in many of the chapters. I realize that my audience mostly finds me through my videos. Some of us don't really like reading, therefore, I won't bore you with blabber. I want to make sure that in each chapter,, or better yet— lesson, in this book, I give you exactly what you're looking for.

I've been called a teacher. I've been called a trainer. I've even been called a coach. Unfortunately, I've never been called a storyteller. My writing style in this book is actually how I get my points across even when talking face to face. Saying all of that to say, it may be a little different from other books you've read. This book is a mix between an instruction manual and a guide. The reason I call it an instruction manual is that I provide you with tactical, step-by-step instructions on how to get certain things accomplished. To some, that may sound like a guide, but it's totally different. Here's my logic behind it. I call this book a guide because through my experiences, failures, pitfalls, and successes, you will be guided to where your focus should lie and what should be avoided. You can think of me, Chastin J. Miles, as your personal tour guide for the duration of this read and through your real estate career. I'm the guy with the lantern right in front of you lighting the path you should walk. When I lead you to the end of our path together, you will have all of the instructions I've given you along the way to take you onto wealth, prosperity, happiness, and success as a real estate agent.

Let's begin.

Part One
My Big Why

Part 1
My Big Why

Why I Decided To Become A Real Estate Agent

I haven't lived in Texas my whole life. I actually moved to Dallas a few years into college. I was born in Houston, you know, the big city down south? My brothers and I grew up as happy as we knew we could be. We pretty much did all the things normal kids do. The only thing that was different about me is that I was intrigued by the thought of owning a business. Even as a small child, I always wanted to start a company of my own . During my adolescent days, I experimented with creating and selling greeting cards, websites, and even clothes made out of newspaper. I guess you can say that I was a pretty creative individual. In my head, I knew one of them would become a success story.

During my freshman year of high school, I moved to a town north of Atlanta by the name of Alpharetta. This is where my real estate story really began. Alpharetta was a very well-established suburb of Atlanta. The town was well established and so was the real estate. I loved riding around and seeing all the big homes in the area. Actually, it was a favorite pastime of mine. I didn't know much about real estate, but I was intrigued by design and architecture. I would love to go into the homes of some of my friends from school and see how different they all were. Big homes, smaller homes, mansions, and townhomes-they were all different. They all had their own creativity. I liked that. Something I would notice while riding around was that most homes were different from one another. It was as if they were all custom homes, which they might have been. At the time, I didn't know if they were or weren't. It just fascinated me to see how different they were.

It wasn't until I got to college that I was introduced to the real estate business. I didn't study real estate or anything. Here's how it all went down. My roommates and I were looking for an off-campus home to live in. One day walking around campus, we saw this advertisement for rental homes. It looked something like this:

This was exactly what we were looking for! Since I was the smart one, they made me call the number. I spoke with a nice lady who took some information from me. She asked me questions like, "What are you all looking for in a home?" and "When were you all looking to move?" I gave her the answers, and she set up a meeting for us to go to her office. The next day, we were all super excited when we showed up at her office, which was really close to campus. When we went inside, there was hardly anyone there. We got a little freaked out, but we still wanted a house. While we were talking to her, I kept getting distracted by all of the posters on the wall. They were advertisements to become a real estate agent. I was intrigued.

She showed us a few homes on a television monitor they had on the wall and asked which ones we wanted to see. We picked two homes from the list that we liked. Next thing you know, she left the room and came back to say, "Ready to check them out?" Immediately we said yes, we were so eager to follow. We felt like such adults. It was crazy!

Next, we hopped in her car which smelt like a freshly smoked cigarette, and she took us to the two homes to show us around. I was hooked on just the process so far. I knew at that moment, this was something I wanted to do with my life. I didn't even know the ends and outs of the business, but I wanted in!

Long story short, we didn't end up getting the rental because we just decided to get an apartment, but I did end up enrolling in real estate classes with her school about a week later. I was in every class, bright and early. I was that guy sitting in the front row in every class. I feel like I did very well in the classes, but I ran out of money. Remember, I was a kid in college. I didn't even tell anyone in my family that I was doing this. I was supposed to be at school getting my degree, and I was skipping class to go to real estate school.

The time came where I had to drop out of real estate school. My money ran out. I will never forget. I told the instructor that I was going to come back after I got my degree but I'm pretty sure he knew it because I had missed my last payment. He boldly told me, "No you won't. That's what everyone says, and they never do."

He was right, I didn't go back.

Well that's not completely true. I didn't go back to that specific school. It wasn't until years later that I re-enrolled in real estate school. This time though, I was doing it back in Texas. My native land. I was also taking classes online this time.

I was extra focused this second go round, and I knew I was going to get my license this time. I still didn't know the ins and outs of the business, but I still wanted it. The little voice in my head just would not let me quit. I took my courses again here in Texas and passed my ever so difficult state exam.

The rest is history.

Today, I'm extremely happy that I made that decision. Having a career in real estate has taught me so much. This is a business that allows me to use all my talents all the time and sometimes at the same time. Yes, there are ups and downs, lots of them, but at the end of the day, I love what I do.

I appreciate your taking the time out to read this book. I want you to learn something from it. I've spent months writing this. I'm going to tell you up front, this is not my first book but this book is really different from my first book. As I said in my first book, it won't be my last. I actually like reading for the most part. When I read books, I always try to learn something from them. When I wrote this, I wanted to make sure I was teaching something.

My story is by no means complete.

In my eyes, this is only the beginning. You are a part of my beginning.

That's enough about me. Now, it's time to get into the real purpose of this book.

Part 1
My Big Why

The Youngest Person In The Room

When I first got into real estate, obviously I was a lot younger than I am now. in fact, I'm still pretty young. Honestly, at the time of writing this, I haven't even hit 30 years old. Being young was always at the forefront of my mind when I first started. I always said, *"Nobody's going to take me seriously."* I knew early on that I needed to learn as much as I could to make this business work. I just remember sometimes when I would meet leads while on listing appointments, I would always get asked the same question. *"So how long have you been doing this?"* Well, it was obvious that I hadn't been doing it my whole life, or 50 years, or 40 years, or 30 years, or anything close to that because I was barely in my 20's. To be exact, I was 23 when I got into the industry, and so I couldn't really say that I had been doing it for a while, but nonetheless, that was a question that I would frequently get asked.

The common objection clients wouldn't want to work with me was the dreaded, *"Well...we would just prefer someone with a little bit more experience."* That crushed me every time because I felt like I was so smart, and I had confidence in my abilities, but the truth of the matter was that it didn't matter to them. They wanted someone with more experience. The ones that would *kind of* take me seriously and *maybe* want to work with me would say things like, *"Do you really know what you're doing?"* It crushed me every time to hear that.

In my head I was thought, "Do you not understand that I had to pass a test for this, *and* I have to be a part of a brokerage?" I would need to explain to them that it's a huge liability for me to even practice real estate because if I mess something up, my broker would get in big trouble. There are so many laws that I was responsible for following and I wanted to make sure I followed all of them. It was almost like the objections never ended. Until, I figured out how to turn it around.

Let me tell you how I overcame some of these objections. The biggest thing that I tried to do was to conduct myself in a professional manner. I wanted my professionalism to be top notch so that there was no question of how long I had been doing this. If I presented, through marketing materials and through a professional and very clean process, they wouldn't look at me like I just popped up out of nowhere.

That was one thing that definitely helped.

Additionally, I had to be extremely knowledgeable. I tried to make sure, and still to this day, I tried to make sure that I was current with everything going on. Not just the market trends but also in marketing, real estate practices, and different laws, so when I'm inevitably asked a question, I will know the answer. Clients are going to ask you questions in the hopes of stumping you. It may be something that they know, and they simply just want to see if you know. To do this, I made sure that I was always attending some type of class, whether it was at my brokerage, at the Board of REALTORS®, or somewhere else because I wanted to ensure that I knew what I was talking about.

Something else I did was practice scripts. This helped in both phone and face-to-face conversations.

There are a lot of commonalities in clients' objections. If you're young, you will start to hear the same things repeatedly, so the scripts really work if you simply practice them. For example, if someone would say, *"So Chastin, how long have you been in real estate?"* I would say, *"Gosh, so long. I can't even remember."* That immediately sends that conversation in a different direction. It's just being quick on your feet, and when you have these scripts internalized, they just flow naturally. Today, they happen naturally because I've done them hundreds of times. Trust me though, you'll be asked this same question. I don't want you to be fearful of being young and working in real estate because it's definitely doable. I'm doing it, and there are tons of other people that are doing it. It just has to start in your head.

Young agents tend to let their thoughts predict the outcome, whether good or bad. We tell ourselves, *"Nobody's going to work with me."* If you're a real estate agent who thinks like that, people won't work with you because you lack confidence about yourself. When you hold your head high in confidence and conduct yourself as the professional that you really are, people will want to work with you even if it's just out of curiosity of your abilities.

Part 1
My Big Why

Question, Is It Hard Being New?

I remember one day I was having lunch with a brand new licensed agent, and he asked me, *"So is this real estate thing hard?"* Honestly, I kind of didn't want to give him the true answer. I mean, I wanted to just say, *"Oh... real estate is so much fun, and it's easy, and you make so much money,"* but my heart just wouldn't let me do that. I decided to answer his question with brutal honesty. Let me just get straight to the point; real estate is hard. It's a very tough career. It's very demanding, especially as a new agent.

I shared with him a simple truth. This is applicable to any new agent, including yourself, but this is what I told him. Read these words carefully and apply them to yourself: **You are a new agent in Dallas, and there are a lot of people in Dallas. As a new agent, you're coming into an industry where there are many other people who do the exact same thing that you do.** He understood what I was saying so there was no further explanation needed. We sat and talked, and he became interested in how I got started. What did I do? Did I have any tips? I didn't really share too much because when I got into the business, I did so many random things just trying to get myself started. That's the biggest reason why real estate is a very tough career to break into. There are so many random things being thrown at you. Out of everything I tried, I learned that you must simply get yourself out there and get started, especially if you don't have a very large network or have clients already lined up. You truly have to go out there and generate business for yourself. He seemed like he understood, but I wasn't quite convinced. Since I opened this can of worms, I figured I'd really start to delve in. By this time, I was damn near preaching to him.

I told him, "You're literally a walking advertisement. Everywhere you go, you're trying to strike up conversation. You're trying to mail out a flyer, print something, or get somebody to trust you with one of the largest purchases or sales of their lives. These are major moments! It's extremely difficult to even get into the business without boldly putting yourself out there.

On the flip side, real estate can be very rewarding, but it's very stressful. There is a lot of time invested into activities that you're not necessarily certain will yield the results that you're looking for. People watch all these real estate shows and see the celebrity agents and the big deals and how fun it looks and yes, there is a fun side. You get to socialize a lot. Eventually, you'll be able to do very large deals and break into that market, but it's one of those careers where you have to put in the work to make that happen.

I wrapped up by telling him:

"If you're up for that challenge, then I say go for it, but don't start a real estate career just because it looks fun to you, and it looks like glamorous on tv. This is a real career. This can even be called a job. If you're a full time agent, you're working from 8:00 or 9:00 in the morning to 9, 10, 11:00, or sometimes even midnight. When you're working, you're working your ass off. All of this work is just so that you can make sure you have money to put food on the table. Here's a big kicker, unfortunately, clients don't necessarily treat you that way. Most times, they make their decision without really taking you into consideration. They don't take into consideration that you have bills to pay and a family to feed, so you've got to be ready for all of those things, and you have to be ready for the ups and downs."

After that spiel, he got the point. Again, I would never say anything to anyone in hopes of crushing their dreams or goals. It's just that I've seen many people come into the business when I did, and they're no longer in the business because no one shared this information with them, so they didn't have the right expectations. They failed.

Going From Broke to 6-Figures

As I begin to tell you more about my journey, I'm taking a
look around at the scenery around me. I am on the balcony
of my high-rise in Dallas. The sun is going down, and you
can see its reflection in the glass of the buildings around
me. It's quite a refreshing sight. If you've ever watched
any of my video blogs, you'll see that I play a time lapse at
the beginning of what I see every morning through the
large glass doors and windows that span from wall to wall.
I get to see the sunrise through the buildings and
everything right from my bedroom. This is my home. The
purpose of me telling you that is not to brag about where I
live or what I have, but to show you what's possible. For
me, it's a constant reminder to remain humble and
recognize where I came from and what my struggles were
getting to this place.

I'll be the first to admit it, I didn't come from the best place.

I didn't have a lot of money. When I got into real estate, there was a time that I depleted all of my money, and I was completely broke. It had gotten so bad that one day I came home to my old apartment, and my lights were off. They weren't off because I forgot to pay the bill. I simply couldn't afford to pay the bill, so they stayed off. I remember opening the refrigerator to make sure my food was still good, but I barely had any food to save so I couldn't really even care much. It was pretty sad actually.

Growing up, I wasn't taught those valuable financial lessons that parents and teachers teach today. I didn't have a savings. I didn't know what a savings was because everybody who I was around lived paycheck to paycheck. I wasn't taught how to manage money because everyone who I was around, didn't have any money, so I didn't really have those lessons, which I feel attributed to the position that I was in because there was a lot that I just didn't learn growing up.

Before I became successful in real estate, I didn't know how to save. I didn't know how to manage my money well, not that there was much to manage, but I knew that I wanted a different outcome for myself. I wanted something better than my current situation.

I got into real estate, spent all my money, and couldn't even keep my electricity on. That truly sucked. It was totally embarrassing. Could you imagine coming home one day after work and realizing your lights are off, and you don't have the money to turn them back on? It's a horrible feeling. I don't blame anyone. I guess I could blame myself, but honestly, I didn't know what I could have done differently. I guess the only thing I could have changed was **not** getting my real estate license.

I look at my life now, being in a place where I don't even have to second guess a bill or second guess a purchase, and it's such a different feeling.

The purpose of this chapter is to give you some lessons that I feel like I've learned along the way in my journey because I realize that all of us are not in a place where we have money flowing in when we start a career in real estate.

Luckily, now I'm in a much better place financially, and of course, I'm still working at it. The difference now is that I'm working hard because I appreciate the things that I have, and I appreciate the lifestyle that I've made for myself. By no means has it always been like this. I'm not even going to pretend that it has. I'm not driving around in a Lamborghini yet, but I do have a very nice car, which is a dream for many. I'm not just going to you, "*Oh, you've got to work hard, and get it.*" Everybody knows that you have to work hard; you have to put in the hours; you have to put in the grunt work; you **HAVE TO WORK HARD**. We all know that, but I feel like there's a few underlying lessons that I really want people to get because these are lessons that I've learned that have been helpful to me and many others.

The first lesson is to *"do you"* and don't worry about anyone else. When I began this journey, I really worried about what people thought. I thought I had to act a certain way, and I thought I had to do things a certain way, and once I shifted that mindset to say, "*Hey Chastin, I'm going to do me. I'm going to do this the way that I need to do it. I'm doing what works for me,*" everything changed. You know, we're not going to be good at everything. You're not going to have everything that the next person has. You need to focus on YOU. Today, I *do me* 100 percent of the time. If there's something that I don't want to do, I say no. If it's something that I do want to do, I'm quick to hop on it, whether it's going somewhere, buying something, taking a trip, or running my business the way that I want to do it. I *do me*. This is an important lesson for everyone. You need to figure out who you are through figuring out your identity and *doing you*. You'll see, that's what's going to make people fall in love with you.

Secondly, you must surround yourself with people who are doing *more* than you. Many people give the advice to surround yourself with likeminded individuals. Well, you've probably also heard that *there are thinkers and there are doers*. A lot of like-minded individuals are just thinkers. They stay in their minds.

Here's what ends up happening. They come up with brilliant ideas, but they don't act on them. I choose to surround myself with people who are actually doing more than what I want to do and more than what I'm currently doing. I choose to be around people who are unknowingly giving me something to push towards. Those are the people who have placed me in situations in which I'm able to network and mingle with the people that they surround themselves with. This ends up putting you in a whole different bracket of people and affiliations, and it really sets you up to do great things that the thinkers, or the people who you may have around you, aren't doing. It's all because they're not thinking on that level.

If you choose to constant be on the same level as everyone around you, you're going to be doing the same things you've been doing, but once you surround yourself with people who are above you, then you start to elevate yourself. This was an important lesson for me and is still my philosophy today.

As I move up the ladder and my income increases, I start buying new cars and toys, but I always have the mindset of elevating. It's okay to ask someone "Who can you introduce me to who may be doing X, Y, and Z because I want to meet that person?" That's a really important thing for anyone in any type of industry. If you want to be great, or if you want to be greater, network with the people who are greater.

Finally, I have learned that you must only focus on where you're trying to go. Let's use the example of going for a drive to your favorite restaurant. When you get into the car, you are focused on going to the restaurant. You're probably very hungry and ready to get something to eat. Since you have that hunger, you are focused on where you are trying to go and you follow through with that mission with no distractions. It's the same thing in business. First, you must know where you're trying to go. This was something that I didn't know for a while. I knew

I wanted a better house. I knew I wanted a fancier car, but what did that look like? Was that a BMW, or was it a Lamborghini? Was that a multi-million-dollar home, or was it a condo in a high rise? If you're wondering why this is important, let me break it down for you. It's essential for you to know what you want because you have got to know what you're going to work towards. You've got to know how much it costs. You've got to know what you have to do to get it. That's how I set my goals. This simple concept is how I'm able to say, "*Okay, I need to make $11,000 this month because that's going to allow me to do X, Y, and Z*".

I'm not working just to work. It's unfortunate, but there are people out there who are just working because they simply want to work. Personally, I'm working to be able to have what I want to have and to get what I want, when I want it. I want to do what I want to do when I want to do it. That's what I like to call FREEDOM.

We all need the freedom mindset. If you're going to work in this business, work towards something. If you can't think of something you want, work towards having freedom. Create the ultimate goal for yourself. Make it something that you can be really satisfied by when you achieve it. Being broke sucks. You have the power to change all circumstances, including your finances.

Not having enough money to buy something to eat sucks. I don't wish that on anybody. If you're currently in that position, now is the moment for you to change it. Get this, the journey hasn't been easy, but if I had to do it all over again, it would probably be a lot easier because I would be more intentional about everything I do including only focusing on what I'm trying to do. This book will help you be intentional with everything. If you're wanting to get into real estate, go ahead and get into real estate. Stop asking yourself if you should. Just do it. If you want to make more money, make more money. Stop asking how to do it. Surround yourself with people who are making a lot of money and you will naturally start to make more money.

I promise you.

I didn't intend for this to be like a rant or anything, but I am passionate about this. Again, It really sucks to be broke, but we all have the power to change that. No matter what your background is. No matter how you grew up. I didn't grow up with money. A lot of my family members still live paycheck to paycheck, and it's their lives, but you can change yours only if you want to. You can create a new legacy for the generations to come.

Part Two
Getting Started Advice

Don't Quit Your Job Just Yet

You probably didn't expect to read this, but I'm going to tell you why you should not quit your job and go into real estate full-time. I know that some of you reading this are probably thinking, *"Why would a Realtor tell me not to quit my job and get into real estate if I want to start real estate?"* The reason is that I'm tired of seeing people crash and burn in this business because they made poor decisions. I'm not implying that it's you or that you're going to be making a poor decision. What I am saying is that some people in this industry are misinforming you of what it's truly like. Agents listen to the wrong person, quit their jobs, and then there's crickets. They literally crash and burn.

Everyday, agents are being misled.

I've heard about people going to interviews at brokerages, and the broker tells them that they can't work real estate part-time, and they need to quit their jobs if they want to join the brokerage. On one hand, I understand their thinking, but on the other hand, you don't have to be a full-time real estate agent to sell a home. You can sell a home as a part-time agent. If any brokerage wants you to quit your job, I hope that they have a good plan for you to get a paycheck very quickly.

I'm going to discuss a couple of reasons why you shouldn't quit your job, but towards the end of the chapter, I will also tell you how you can transition to being a full-time agent, without just diving in, because there's definitely a smarter way to do it. This chapter is not for those of you who have saved up a lot of money, whether it's six months worth or a year. This isn't for you because you're covered. You have money in the bank; you have that cushion, but a lot of people, including myself, when I got into the business, aren't covered. So for whom is this chapter?

I'm writing to those of you whom are literally thinking about jumping into this business full-time without a plan or without that cushion of money. Like I said, people have been misinformed, and I want to make sure that I cover this topic.

The first reason shouldn't quit your job to do real estate full-time is because you don't necessarily know if real estate is truly for you. I know a lot of people see the career and see the industry from the outside, but you don't really know if you're going to like it once you get in it. It can be deceiving because you see a lot of the fancy cool pictures and videos. Remember I said that this can be a very glamorous career? I wasn't lying but, you don't see a lot of the things that go on behind the scenes, and that's why I try to be so transparent and really give you the reality of what the real estate industry is like. Honestly, before I got into it, I didn't think that I would even be doing half of the things that I'm doing now.

I remember a time in college when I needed a job badly, and my roommate had just gotten a job at the local sporting goods store. He came home one night practically banging down my door. He knew I needed a job and started shouting, "*You need to go up there. They are hiring on the spot.*" I was like WTF? He went on to tell me that this store by the mall was hiring. So, I went up there a couple of days later and filled out an application, and they called me in for an interview. I aced the interview, of course. Well, I wouldn't really say that I aced it. I think that they were just needing people to work there, so they offered me a job.

I went in on my start date, and I completed the training program in a few days, and then it was time for me to go out onto the floor and work my first full shift. I worked that shift from clock in to clock out. I put clothes on hangers, folded dry fit shirts, and answered the phone every time it would ring my department. The next day, I showed up, but I didn't make it inside the store. I stayed in the parking lot. I sat in my car and with a deep sigh, I attempted the inevitable. I called them from my cellphone and told him that I wasn't coming in for my shift. The nice manager on the phone quickly asked, *"Are you sick, are you okay? What's going on?"* I could tell she was truly concerned, after all, I was a model trainee.

I answered her with my well thought out response by saying *"No, it's just not gonna work."* She didn't understand what I was saying. I mean, I wasn't really doing a good job explaining myself. I had never really done this before, so I just flat out said, *"I'm not coming back to work."* She understood it that time. I didn't have a true reason but that was my first true experience at recognizing something that just wasn't for me. I didn't like the job and I couldn't do it for even one more day.

Granted, I was going to get a paycheck, and it was probably going to be an easy job, but it just wasn't for me. This was truly an instance when I realized that you don't really know if a job or a career is for you until you actually get into it and start working in it.

The same is true with real estate; once you get into the business, then and only then, if you really decide that it is for you, it's way more appropriate to quit your job. Just don't quit your job ahead of time without even experiencing a day in the life as a real estate agent. Think about the reason that you got a job. Initially, you got a job because you needed money, and real estate is no different. Most decide to do real estate because they want to make money. What if I tell you you're going to need money to even run a real estate business. Would you still be ready to quit your job?

I even tell people sometimes that they'll probably spend more money in their first year than they'll make. When you're working real estate full time, it's different from going into a job. You're not locked down to a location, which means you're driving all the time. That results in spending more money in gas. You have to go out and entertain people, so you're spending more money on lunches and food, not to mention all of the business expenses that you're going to incur: Real Estate license, business cards, signs, etc. All of that stuff costs money but it's necessary. This is not a career for someone to go into when you don't have any money. If you have a job, and you have money coming in, then yeah, you can pay for the licenses, you can pay for the classes, you can pay for the materials, you can pay for the entertaining and everything else that accompanies this. On the other hand, if you don't have ANY money, you're not going to make it very far.

Another reason that you should keep your job is that a job can put you in a position to give you those first few contacts that could turn into a real estate deal. If you're somewhere where you're interacting with employees, you're interacting with customers; you're interacting with a lot of people. These people can be the connections to get your real estate business going. Think about this: When you quit your job and you don't have those contacts anymore, you're literally by yourself, so you're going to have to create those contacts out of nowhere by probably going out and meeting all new people or cold calling. I understand that not everybody is the type of person to go out and strike up a conversation with people, but at your job you're probably more comfortable with the people you work with, and you have a connection with them. You can let those be your first referral sources or better yet, even your first clients. I remember back when I was working, I still kept in contact with a lot of my colleagues, and many of them have become clients of mine or they've been good referral sources. You just never know, so you don't want to burn those bridges.

You will get to a point in your real estate career when it is time for you to quit your job. You will have saved up some money, and you can make that move. There will be a time when you've gotten too busy with your real estate business, and you have money coming in. Don't think that you're going to have to do both for a very long time. As long as you bust your butt while you're trying to rev up your real estate business, you'll be able to quit your job in no time. There's no real urgency to do it immediately. The one that you're going to be doing as a new agent, especially as a brand-new agent, is learning. You're just going to be training and reading and going to classes. It's not going to fill up a full eight-hour work day, and for the most part, you won't even know how to fill your schedule for the full eight to twelve hours.

If you have that availability, go ahead and keep your job. Keep some money coming in. Don't worry; it's only temporary, and it's not going to be forever. My advice for those of you who are working a job and who want to transition into real estate full-time is to start off with adjusting your schedule. If you're working a full-time job right now, go down to part-time if it's possible. That will allow you to work real estate and work your job at the same time.

You want to start cutting back on your spending. Stop spending like you know another paycheck is coming in two weeks. Get out of that mentality because once you do go into real estate full time, you can't think like that at all, so you may as well just practice now. Just cutting your spending back to where you're not spending so much so often can really help you start to save up that cushion of money to leave your job.

Speaking of saving up, start to build that cushion. I recommend three to six months of savings to carry you over if you don't have a closing, or if the market is slow, or your business is slow. Whatever the reason may be, your savings of money can really help you out. Plus, if you're doing this alongside becoming a real estate agent, you're going to start to prepare for the things that you'd have to pay for as a new agent, and you can be prepared and actually afford those necessities.

Getting The Title

Sometimes, I feel like nobody's telling the full story about what it's like to become a Realtor. There's a lot of videos and articles out there, and for the most part, they all say the same things. Yes, we know you have to get your real estate license, but what about everything else? Let me ask you this. Are you someone who is considering getting your real estate license and have been doing a lot of research? Do you feel like you know everything that you need to do so? I find this to be a very interesting topic, which is why I've dedicated a whole chapter to it.

If you've watched my YouTube channel, you know I like to provide you with information about what it's like *actually* working in real estate. Basically, I like to show you the reality of the real estate career from an agent's perspective. I oftentimes say the things that nobody wants to hear or nobody else wants to tell you because they're scared for one reason or another. I just always told myself- this is stuff that people really need to know which is why I started my channel, do my videos, and write books like this. Be sure to pay close attention. Getting the actual title is to big goal.

Here's what you've probably been told, this is the track that most people send you down. They say go to real estate school, *obviously*, get your license, *obviously*, and then start selling. That's pretty much it. What about all the other steps? Honestly, I feel like if I would've known some of the other steps before, I could have saved myself a lot of time and money.

When I got into real estate, I went to two different real estate schools. As you know from before, I was working with my roommates, and we were living on campus for school and decided that we wanted to move off campus for obvious reasons. We wanted to get our own place. We were all partiers, and we wanted to escape the rules of the school.

When I enrolled in that first school, little did I know that it was one of the more expensive schools for no apparent reason. Nobody really told me that there were cheaper options. As you know, I dropped out, of course. I ended up picking up a few years later, which was a long time, but I had a little money saved up, and I was ready the 2nd time. However, the second time I ended up going to a different school that was a lot cheaper, but it was the same exact information.

That was kind of interesting to me, and I wondered why nobody told me that there were other options out there. Just one of those things that I didn't know. It's true that you are required get your license, but it's not true that you have to get it from any certain school. There's a lot of different real estate schools out there for you to choose from, but we will get into the different schools a bit later.

There's so much that people don't tell you. Even after you have gotten through the course at the real estate school, there is a final exam you must take. Then there's an actual state exam, that you have to pass before you finally get your license. Those are two different exams that could come off seeming like they are one.

Here's another hidden fact. Along the way, they will be charging you for certain things. For me, it almost got to a point where I couldn't even take the state exam because there were things that I had to pay for before I could even take the state exam. I was like, *"Dang! Why didn't y'all tell me this ahead of time?"* (Excuse my Texas accent.) I probably would have reconsidered my whole career path or waited for a different time, but being the type of person that I am, the entrepreneur that I am, I figured it out and scraped up the money for it. Again, one of those things that nobody told me. I didn't know that getting a real estate license was a hefty investment in itself.

After I got my license, there was the whole brokerage thing. You've probably seen someone jump from agency to agency to agency. The reason they do that is that there are so many options out there, and there are so many things that you just don't know yet. You're so excited about getting your license and getting started, and you end up taking one recommendation from someone and end up at a place that isn't necessarily right for you. This is a major problem in the industry.

Are you someone who's in that position right now? You are deciding to become a real estate agent, you know you want to get into the business for one reason or another, but you feel like there are questions that are unanswered, or you need some guidance, or you just really need someone to show you the way. If that's you, you're in for a real treat. Not only does this book give you a lot of information, but I am also going to give you access into a special resource that I designed. It's called Future Agent Academy. This is a database full of resources to provide the answers you are looking for. Since you purchased this book, I'm going to give you free access. Simply visit www.futureagentacademy.com and enter the code *theRealb4* to get free access.

What You Can Do Before You Actually Get Your License

I realize that a lot of my audience and even some of you who may be reading this aren't necessarily licensed yet, and that's why I decided to include this chapter. This chapter is strictly for people who are making that transition into real estate, whether you're in real estate school or still deciding whether you want to become a real estate agent. I'm going to share with you what you can be doing in the meantime so that when you get your state license, you're steps ahead and you're ready to hit the ground running.

The first thing you're going to need when you become a real estate agent is a network. I'm not talking about a WIFI network or a computer network, I'm talking about a network of people. Your network is going to eventually bring you your net-worth. I recommend that you start building your personal network of people even before you get your real estate license. This is going to come in handy so that when you get your license, you have people to tell that you're a real estate agent. Informing your network of your new career path is going to be your first official task as an agent. This is one thing that I wish I would've done before I got into the business. I kind of started fresh and didn't really have anyone apart of my network, so I couldn't really announce it to the world that I was in real estate because there was no one to announce it to.

When I got my license, it was in a city where I had never lived, and I didn't have any friends. Therefore, I recommend that you go out and start attending events, whether that's parties, clubs, business networking events, restaurants, whatever you like to do. I recommend that you go out and start meeting new people. It doesn't have to be all about business, but start making friends so that when you do get into real estate, you have a network of people there ready to support you simply because they like you. This is going to carry you very far in your real estate career, so definitely get out there and start meeting people ahead of time.

The next thing that I recommend for you to do is to choose a brokerage. You don't have to go as far as interviewing but at least become familiar with your options ahead of time. You want to go ahead and choose where you're going to work. When you become a real estate agent, it's not very fun to have a lag time in between getting your license and beginning to work. You can alleviate this by doing your homework on brokerages and agencies ahead of time. You're going to read all about real estate brokerages and how you can choose a real estate broker, so I recommend that you continue to pay close attention. This is something that you can do even before your license is active. Most real estate companies out there want you to interview with them. They want to tell you all about their company and why you should work with them. It's not going to hurt if you have some extra time during the week or on the weekends. Go out there and interview with companies to simply see who you may want to work for once you get your real estate license.

The last thing I recommend that you do ahead of time, like I said before, is start getting in the mindset of saving money. Real estate is a 100% commissioned career, so you need to know how to manage your money. Again, you want to have some type of cushion there. You're going to read about the typical expenses of new real estate agents, but you're going to want to have some money there so that when you do get licensed, you can pay for things that you need to pay for. Expenses will include marketing, mentoring, materials, supplies, more coaching, and so on. You've got to have some money there, especially if you're transitioning from a job into working real estate full-time. I repeat, you're going to need to have some money saved.

The Options In This Business

I can't complain; business has been good the last few years. Actually, business has been great, and I wish it to be the same for you. What I want to get across to you is the different options you have to make money with your real estate license. I'm going to specifically present to you five different jobs that you can have with your real estate license. I'm going to go over some of the common ones and then some roles you may not have considered. Everything that I'm telling about in this chapter, you can do only when you become licensed. There are so many opportunities out there with ways that you can make money in the real estate business. You're not just limited to the conventional routes that most new licensees decide to take.

The first role is fairly common. This is going to be the role of your standard buyer's agent or listing agent. I'm going to combine these into one because they are extremely similar. What a buyer's agent does is work with potential home buyers to help them buy a home. You take them through the financing process, you show them properties, and you facilitate their contract to close. Some people solely do this 100% of the time in their business.

There's also a listing agent. The listing agent does the same thing, but they work with listings. When we say *Listings,* we are referring to people who are wanting to sell their homes. So instead of working with a buyer, you're working with a home owner. Typically, agents who are working as listing agents really like to market properties. They like to put them on the market or bring them to the public eye. They really like to create a big presentation when marketing properties. A listing agent will take the listing and put the home on the Multiple Listing Service or MLS, market it, and work hard to get it sold. They pretty much do everything needed to get it sold, but they also must perform the contract to close procedures.

It's also common for an agent to work as a buyer's agent and a listing agent at the same time. When I first got into the business, I just wanted to make money, so I didn't discriminate. Whatever came my way, I took it! It didn't matter if it was a listing or a buyer.

What ends up happening most times is new agents work with buyers first because that's just how it tends to happen. It's not a rule or anything, but a lot of new agents tend to gravitate towards buyers just because they're a little bit easier than listings. Something to note though is that buyers could take longer to close, but listings also have their challenges. You can choose to do whatever you want to do in the business, but buyer's agents and listing agents are two of the common roles that you'll see a lot of people use their licenses for.

Alongside buyer's agents and listing agents are going to be your builder's agents. Sometimes, we call these agents new construction salespersons. Builder's agents typically work exclusively for homebuilders. As a builder's agent, you'll probably be placed in an office or a model home. You're going to help the people who walk in the door. Your job will consist of showing the homes, telling them about the actual product, showing the different floor plans or *elevations*, and facilitating the buyer's contract to close process.

As the builder's representative, sometimes you are going to work alongside a buyer's agent from another brokerage. An example of this is that when a buyer walks in the door, they could already have an agent. In your position, you're not necessarily the listing agent or the buyer's agent. You are strictly the builder's representative. At the end of the day, you are an agent, so you still get paid.

As a builder's representative you may be operating on a different pay scale, however. What does that mean? It simply means you may receive a different commission than a normal buyer's agent. The flip side of that is, as a builder's agent, you get a lot of walk in traffic! If the client doesn't have an agent, then that's pretty much your client for the duration of the transaction.

It's not necessarily hard to get a job as a builder's agent. A lot of builders like working with agents, especially the big box builders. It may be a little bit more difficult if you're trying to work for a custom builder, but if you're going to one of the big mass-producing builders, you can simply visit their website and see any job positions they have open. You can see what they're hiring for as well as what the position pays. Most of the time, it will pay a salary, and if you're lucky, a commission on top of that.

There are also leasing agents. In my videos, I talk about leases a lot because I think that they are a phenomenal way for an agent to generate business and start making money early on. That's honestly why I created a whole program around it called Rental Boss. I wanted to show real estate agents how to work leases. In my program, I show them how to attract rental clients and how to get paid so that they can get some money in their pockets while trying to get buyers and sellers. Leasing agents tend to work exclusively with leases, meaning rentals. I personally know some amazing agents who have built a whole business around just leases.

When I first joined my old Keller Williams office, there was a new agent who had signed on shortly after I joined. There was something different about this woman though. She got her own office! I knew she was someone important; I just didn't know who she was. Having an office was a big deal at this firm. There weren't many of them. Months passed before I said a word to her. I always thought, *What would I say? Why would I say anything?* Then one day, out of nowhere, we talked. It turned out, she had a leasing company. She told me she had recently moved her family and her company to Dallas from Houston, TX. I was fascinated. I wasn't necessarily fascinated with her doing leasing, but I was fascinated by the fact that she had a whole company built around this. She was young, friendly, popular, and rich! We became great friends, and we are still great friends today. I recently interviewed her on how her business was going, and her results were astonishing. She has a huge staff, and by huge, I mean 10 or 12 people. They all make thousands and thousands of dollars a month. I'm talking, at least $30,000 on autopilot. By the time of this interview, I knew there was big money in leasing, I just didn't know many agents who were making big things happen and building businesses around leasing.

You can make a lot of money, and most of the time, it takes half the effort that a conventional sale takes. As a leasing agent, you can build a whole business around rentals, or you can work on a team just as their exclusive leasing agent. As a leasing agent, you're typically not going to do sales. If you wanted to, you could do a sale if somebody wants one because your license allows you to do it, but you're mostly centered around doing leases. Helping people find apartments and rental homes is your #1 job. The fun part about doing leases is that you're getting them in and out, so it's typically a pretty quick and easy process.

The fourth role that I want to talk about is that of a commercial real estate agent or commercial broker. Commercial agents are agents who work exclusively with commercial properties. By commercial I mean retail stores, office buildings, restaurants, gas stations, etc. Basically, anything that's not a residential or multifamily home.

As I'm writing this, I'm sitting in an office building. This is considered a commercial property, so as a commercial agent, you could lease me this space. You can lease the whole building out. You can even broker a deal to build a whole office development on a piece of land. That's just a small piece of what commercial agents can do.

There is BIG money in the commercial real estate industry. I don't work in commercial because it is a whole different ballgame, but your real estate license will allow you to work with commercial properties. I typically don't recommend that you do both. You should choose one side; residential or commercial. A lot of clients that you're going to be working with don't typically like you to dabble in both sides. When I tell you it's two different worlds, I mean different everything: different contracts, different negotiations, different lengths of the processes, and different pay structures. In commercial, everything is different, but the good thing is that having a real estate license enables you to work as a commercial agent if you want. If you have a friend or family member who wants you to broker their commercial deal, or if you decide to become an exclusive commercial agent where all you do is commercial, you have the ability to do it.

The last job I'm going to tell you about that you can do with your license is the role of a property manager. Unlike a leasing agent, a property manager *manages* the whole property. Most of the time, you see property management companies or property management agents managing multifamily properties, such as huge apartment complexes or even small as duplexes or a single family home. A property manager is the one who makes sure that everything is going as it should with that multifamily development or property.

The role of a property manager is very important to the community, especially when there are many tenants involved. There's rent that needs to be collected, evictions that need to be filed, tenants that need a place to live, and repairs that need to be made. Anything that goes on with that multifamily development is the responsibility of a property manager.

You can get a job as a property manager or even start your own property management company. The one thing about property management is that it's not a pretty or glamorous role. As a property manager, you deal with a lot of problems that people have. You're the one that gets those angry phone calls from tenants. You're the one will have to chase down people for money and unfortunately, you're the one that will put people out of their homes. It's a role that requires a person to have thick skin and not have your emotions affecting your day to day decisions.

Your license will allow you to do any one of those five roles. For purposes of this book, those are the five common roles that I've identified that I wanted to present to you. There are so many other roles you can take with your real estate license. You can see a snapshot of these different roles below.

Like what...?

- Buyers Agent
- Listing Agent
- Property Manager
- Commercial Agent
- Team Leader/Manager
- Coach/Trainer
- Showing Agent

- Real Estate Assistant
- Leasing Agent
- Investor
- BPO
- New Home Salesperson
- Consultant
- Government

In my Future Agent Academy database that I mentioned earlier in the book, I do go over the 14 different roles that you can work with your real estate license.

The purpose of this chapter is to get you thinking about what role you want to play in the real estate industry. If you want to just be a buyer's agent, or a listing agent, or if you want to go down the commercial route or the property management route. Regardless, there are options, so you don't necessarily have to be limited.

Go with whichever one you feel good doing, the one you think you will have a passion for. Something about commercial that draws a lot of people to it is that commercial is not very emotional. Everybody dealing with commercial properties are mostly focusing on the numbers, the return on investment, occupancy rates, and so on. Therefore, people who don't want to deal with emotions like commercial.

Others like property management because they get to really play by a strict set of rules. It's not going outside of boundaries, and there are clear lines through rental agreements. There's a clear set role, but property management can have a lot of headaches. You really must be a strong, thick skinned individual to be a property manager. I would encourage you to research everything that's available to you in this industry and really see how you want to put your license to work.

Transitioning to 100% Commission

Transitioning from a full-time income to a commission-based income is in many ways scary. There are so many different objectives when you are transitioning from working a full-time job, with a steady income, to working a 100% commissioned role. You need to be prepared and know how you can make this transition as smooth as possible. I want to share my personal thoughts on how you can make this transition and what you can be prepared for when you are coming from a full-time or part-time job. This information can really go for any type of full- time commission sales job or a role as an independent contractor in a company, so it should be helpful for just about anyone considering this.

First, let me just say, there is one thing that keeps people from performing at their full potential. Have you had that feeling where there was always something heavy on your shoulders? This feeling is similar. It's so scary to even think about not knowing where your next paycheck is going to come from or when it's coming. When you are a fully commissioned employee or independent contractor, you really don't know what's around the corner until you get there. You are completely responsible for how much money you make and if you make money or not. To be honest with you, most sales jobs are 100 percent commissioned jobs. If you're lucky, some of them may have small salaries attached to them, but for the most part, if you're working in sales, such as real estate, you're going to be on a 100 percent commission pay structure.

Don't think I'm crazy for saying this, but I actually prefer working on commission because that way my earning potential is unlimited. I can make as much money as I want to make, therefore I can really control my lifestyle instead of having my lifestyle controlled by a salary.

One thing that I realized when I left my full-time job was that I turned into an ultimate hustler. You're probably wondering, what is an *ultimate hustler*? An ultimate hustler is someone who is doing whatever it takes , at all times, to make a living. It's like you end up transitioning into this whatever-it-takes kind of person when you're working. That's what I call *ultimate grind mode*. You literally WANT to do whatever it takes to make a dollar at the end of the day. Even today, I'm still in that whatever-it-takes mode, and you really learn how to sell yourself or sell your product or service, really good. You really begin to work harder than ever. I'm sure you're a hard worker right now, especially if you're working a job, but this is different. What you will notice is a different type of hard work overall. The hard work that I'm referring to is the work you put in to make people say yes to you. Your money becomes tied to that one word. At the end of the day, whether you eat or not is based solely upon your sales abilities and someone telling you *yes*. Now hear me out, you need to be smart about the decision to leave your job. Although I do believe that anything is possible, you should still put some serious thought behind it. If you know that you are one flat tire away from being put out on the street, do not quit your job. That's an example of a decision that's just not wise.

Really begin considering all factors and count your money. Do you currently have three to six months of savings? When I started, I had about two and a half months of savings. It was quickly depleted, but I would say a healthy starting number would be three months because I know that six months is unrealistic for a lot of people.

If you read my story, you'll see that I learned a lot. It took me going completely broke to set myself up in a different way. I don't regret it, and I wouldn't change it because it was a learning lesson. This chapter is not really about my story, but again, I don't regret my decisions.

Think about all of your responsibilities and your obligations. If you have a partner or if you have children or a family to take care of, really take all that into account and see if it's the best decision for you to make this type of jump.

Come up with a plan that's going to work for you and your personal situation. I can't tell you exactly what that plan is but come up with a plan. Only you can do this because it's tied to your personal finances.

The next thing that you want to be ready to do is to cut back and live below your means. When I was guaranteed a paycheck, I was doing anything and everything that I wanted to do. Granted I was living paycheck to paycheck, which definitely wasn't the smartest thing, but I still knew that I had money coming in, so why not? On most of my off days, you could find me at the mall, buying expensive brands and loads of things that I just didn't need. I was blowing money all over the place just because I had it, and I knew that if I spent it all, I still had a paycheck coming that Friday. I didn't learn these valuable lessons that I'm telling you until I went 100 percent commission. I had to cut out a lot of the eating out, the shopping, the trips. Pretty much all of my money went towards bills and my business because that was my only concern. Now, I'm not saying you can't live your life, or you must save 100% of your money; I'm simply saying to cut back. Look at your bank statements and see what areas you can make cuts in. Ask yourself, what's not necessary for your existence? When I did this, I realized that my necessities were all I really had room for.

You will realize that everything becomes all about building the business. Real estate is a business that you just took a huge leap of faith to get into. You really have got to learn how to budget your money and budget your paychecks better before you quit, because when you're working 100 percent commission, it's extremely difficult to budget and save. You can't continue to live paycheck to paycheck like you still have a job and have another paycheck coming in. You're going to need to plan your financial moves well in advance.

Here's something that will help you decide how much money you need to live each month. Think about your bills, your expenses, and whatever debts you have. Add all of those up and calculate the minimum amount of money that you need per month. When you have that number, multiply it by 3. This number is going to tell you how much money you need to make per month.

Still with me?

Now we will break that money up into its appropriate places. One third of it is going to go towards your living expenses. This includes your rent or mortgage, your car note, bills, everything you calculated before. The next third is going to go into a savings account. I would recommend a money market account for this. That way you can begin to invest this money and have it make returns for you. The final third, you can use that for your spending money to do whatever you want to do. Later in this book, I'm going to tell you how to make your first $100,000 a year in real estate so you can actually have money to do this with. This will be an important chapter because the number that you need will most likely increase. We will come up with a number that takes your business expenses into account, so you don't have to use your personal money as your business expense money.

Let's break down that personal money and savings even more. I mentioned having a money market account that will allow you to make investments with your savings. I didn't automatically know this when I started making money. Keep in mind, I had no previous financial training or knowledge. One day, one of my friends put me in touch with her financial planner, and I figured it was a good time for me to have a meeting. I knew that there was a way to make money work for me. Especially when I started to have thousands of dollars just sitting in my checking account. When you get ready to start making investments, or you want to create other opportunities with your money, I would do the same thing. Ask for recommendations and schedule a meeting to speak with a financial planner that can help you map out what you can do with the money that you bring in so that you are making smarter investment decisions.

Working on commission can make you a very wealthy individual, but you've got to know how to do it, and you've got to know how to manage your money. If you make good financial decisions with the money that you make, I'm telling you, you can literally have it all.

Like anything great, it's not going to be easy. It's going to be scary as hell jumping into 100 percent commission, but once you get your rhythm going and once you've experienced it, there's no turning back. I can't even imagine myself going to get a job ever again. You're going to get to that place, but it's going to take that leap of faith. If you follow the guidance in this book and you really take in what I say, it could make that transition a lot easier.

Your (Not Such A) Realtor Salary

If you're still considering joining the real estate industry and you're thinking, *"Chastin, c'mon man, how much money will I be making?"* Maybe you are currently in real estate, and you want to know how much money you *should* be making. This chapter will be speaking directly to you.

I've been in real estate for many years now and sold millions and millions of dollars-worth of real estate every single year, and it's produced a good salary for me.

Before I really dive deep into it, just note, I don't want to overwhelm you. I want to be as clear as possible, so feel free to reread whatever you need to so that you are able to grasp the information that I will present to you.

NAR, the National Association of REALTORS®, states that the average realtor salary, or the average amount of money that a Realtor makes every year. is around $42,500. I know that number may seem exciting to some people, but just wait. I want to tell you how that's broken down and how it typically works because, believe it or not, most agents don't make anywhere near that,

As I stated earlier, it's most common for an agent to be 100 percent commissioned. Most of the time, if you have a salaried real estate position, you're working for a company, or you're working on a team, and you're not acting as a Realtor, meaning that you're not getting new clients and taking them from acquisition to close. You're basically doing whatever you're told. In a salaried real estate position, you're most likely working for someone, and they are paying you a salary. You're basically building their business and not building your own. I wanted to point that out because there are salaried real estate opportunities out there, but that's not what this chapter is about.

This chapter is about you actually working as a real estate agent and getting paid from your personal real estate deals. I said that most agents in the real estate industry work off of commission, so let me break down what commission is. For those of you who don't know; typically, in a job you're going to have an hourly wage, or you're going to have a salary. Hourly, meaning from the time you clock in to when you clock out, you're going to get paid a certain dollar amount. You're getting paid dollars for hours. A salary means you're going to get paid a certain amount of money per year, no matter how much or how little you work. In a salaried position, this is the set number that is disclosed to you, and this is what you're going to get at the end of the year. Most people who I know that work a salary end up working way more than the average 40-hour workweek. When you get paid commission, you're only getting paid for what you produce or what you sell. If you're not selling, you're not making money.

In a commissioned sales position, there is no hourly or salary guarantees. There isn't that type of security there that can make you feel comfortable knowing that you're going to bring a certain amount of money home. It's literally all on you. Unlike a job, when you are working commission, everything that you make as income, must be accounted for. You've got to account for your own taxes, your own marketing expenses, your own transportation, your own everything. You've got to pay for everything in your business. There is nobody giving you a lot of the things that a job normally would. You don't get uniforms, supplies, paid time off, insurance benefits, 401k, or anything like that. This makes most people uncomfortable. For me, I was uncomfortable with it at first, but today it's all I really know. Now I honestly couldn't even see myself going back to an hourly or salaried position over working commission.

You literally can make as much money as you want.

Having said that, I want to break down how the actual pay structure works as a commissioned real estate agent.

When you close a deal, you're going to get a percentage of the sales price of the home that you sell. For example, if you sell $100,000 home, you're going to get a percentage of that as your "commission." That's not the end though; there are these little things called splits involved. As a real estate agent, you're going to work at a brokerage or agency, and you're going to have a broker who's managing your license. The broker is there to train you, help you, provide you with what's needed, and most importantly, ensure you're not breaking any laws. The broker is the big umbrella over you, protecting you from the big storm. The broker is going to provide you with some resources, with training, with the company marketing, probably an office space, amongst other things.

In return for a broker doing these things for you, they want to get paid, so they do that by taking a split of your commission. That's where that word *split* comes from. When you get a commission from the sales price of a home, you're going to split it with your broker. That amount can vary by whatever brokerage you are an agent at. There are brokers who offer a 100 percent split, which means you get 100 percent of the gross commission on the sale. This means they don't take any money off from your commission. With 100% brokers, you may have to pay a transaction fee or a monthly fee. It's common to see some brokerages having lower splits and some have higher splits, so when you're interviewing, they're going to let you know ahead of time what their splits are to be an agent at their firm.

When you sell a home, if you are representing one party, meaning you are only representing either the buyer or the seller, the typical commission that you receive from a sale is going to be 3%. If you represent both sides, it tends to be 6%. Commission is a negotiated amount, but it's pretty standard to see 3% as the amount that you'll take home *before* your broker split.

Back to the example of the $100,000 home, representing one side. If you sell a $100,000 home, you're going to receive a commission of $3,000 before your broker split. Whatever your broker split is, you can just deduct that from that $3,000. The difference is the number you're going to put into your pocket. With that final number, you need to account for your taxes, insurance, marketing expenses, and so on.

The only way to make money in the real estate business is to sell. You must sell properties. If you're not closing on homes, you're not making money. You need to be working with buyers, and you need to be working with sellers. You can work with tenants looking for a lease, if you are working a good number of them, but you've still got to be closing deals to make the big money. Just because you're a real estate agent, and you have a real estate license, does not mean you're going to automatically make money. That's where a lot of agents fail in the business. The agents that fail don't really understand that it's essential to get out there and work for it. It's not just going to fall into your lap because you've gotten your license.

This is where we get into finding your own clients and getting them to execute a contract. Once you get them

to close on a home, then and only then, will you get that
paycheck.

Part Three
Pick Your Side

Agents vs. Brokers

REALTOR®, real estate agent, real estate associate, real estate salespersons assistant; these are all terms that you've probably heard of if you've done any type of looking into the real estate industry or even if you received a business card from another real estate agent. They're all different roles within the real estate business. Some of them do the same things, and some of them don't. If you're curious about what they mean and what they do, that's what this chapter is about. Basically, what's the difference with those distinctions and titles? I want to take a moment and just point out two of them, specifically in this chapter, because these two are the most common, in my opinion. The two we will go over are the real estate agent and the broker.

Something to note, I'm not promoting a specific broker. I just want to give you a better understanding.

In my current role, I am what you would call a real estate agent. I have completed all the licensing and courses needed to get my real estate license to be able to sell real estate. I mainly help buyers, sellers, tenants, landlords, and run my team. Granted, I can do any number of things with my license, but my actual title is a real estate agent. Alongside this title, I also have the REALTOR® distinction, so I can also be called a Realtor. We will get into the differences of these a little later.

In my business, I work for a real estate broker. The broker holds my real estate license and is essentially responsible for my practicing of real estate. You must belong to a broker, so my license is held by a broker or brokerage. You've probably seen big companies out there like Keller Williams, Century 21, Coldwell Banker, EXP, RE/MAX, Sotheby's and some of the other big brands. These are real estate brokerages, and each one of these offices is licensed by a broker.

A broker signed his or her name on the line, accepting responsibility for the specific office, which in turn means, "*I'm going to be responsible for these agents.*" Basically, a broker is someone who is the liable party for the actions that the agents take.

Not to confuse you, but I will say, there are differences between a broker and an actual owner. In most offices, the broker is the owner, but it's not uncommon to see that the broker and the owner are two separate people. That basically means that there is a broker who is still that responsible liable party, and there's someone that actually runs the office or may have put up the money for the office and owns the brand name. You don't have to be an owner to be a broker and vice versa. You can be both, or you can take one or the other.

One big thing with brokers is that brokers must go through a lot more education than just a normal Realtor or a real estate agent. Most of the time, a broker has been in the business for a longer period of time, and they have a lot of experience. To become a broker, one has to take what's known as the broker's exam, which from my understanding, is like 10 times harder than the regular salesperson exam. Prospective brokers must have that knowledge and have that education to be able to pass that exam. Here in Texas, they also require that you have been in business for a certain amount of years before you can even apply for your broker's license, so that's one thing to take into consideration. In some states, it's pretty common for agents to be referenced to as brokers but don't let that trick you because there's still that education requirement for you to be a true broker, so you can manage and sponsor other agents.

The easiest way to wrap your head around this is knowing that brokers are typically more educated and more responsible and have been in the business for a lot longer, so they have experienced a lot more than your standard real estate agent.

Some real estate agents can be in the business for a very long time and choose to never get their broker's license. For me, I don't have my broker's license, and I'll talk to you very soon about why I haven't gone down that road yet. It's something that some agents get into the business to do. They get into the business to be an agent for their whole career, while some take the road where they want to become a broker and manage other agents.

There is another title also known as an associate broker or broker's associate. A broker's associate is someone who has gotten their broker's license, but they still work for another broker. You have the big broker as the head, and then you have the broker's associate right below them. Below the broker associates, you'll have the actual salespeople.

A broker associate is someone that does have that education, passed the test, and put that time in, but they're not choosing to open their own brokerages or manage other agents. You can only open a brokerage and bring those agents if you have your broker's license, unless you're just going to become the financial partner in an office. There needs to be a broker in place to manage those licenses. Any money that comes in for you, as an agent, is going to be made out to the broker, and in turn the broker pays you.

Every listing that you take, even though it's your listing, is under the broker's name because the broker is the responsible person for everything that you do in real estate. If you haven't taken your real estate tests yet, this is a big part of it because you're required to know what things you can do as an agent and what things that you must have your broker's license to do.

You don't want to get caught slipping, doing something that you have no business doing because the Real Estate Commission will come after you. You must make sure even in your marketing and advertising or in bringing in other agents or assistants to your team that you're not representing yourself as someone that you are not, such as a broker. There are certain things that you as an agent can do, and there are other things that you're required to have a broker's license to do. Just be sure, especially if you're about to take your real estate exam.

I repeat, be sure to know the differences of these things.

I hear a lot of people talk about becoming a broker because they think that there's more money in being a broker, and that can be true, especially if you are going to be bringing on agents, but it's also a huge financial risk and liability. This is a reason why I have not taken the plunge to become a broker yet. I will be going down the road to get my broker's license and acting as a broker-associate, but I don't have any immediate plans of opening my own firm. When you get into opening your own firm and bringing on agents, the agents typically don't like their broker to sell real estate. That will begin to take me away from what I really set out to do, and I'm simply not ready for that.

Granted, I know that I would be a great broker, but I have more work to do before I choose to become one.

People who decide to open brokerages make a huge financial investment in doing so. It's like opening a restaurant franchise or a retail store. You are starting from the bottom in hopes of the business being successful.

Agents vs. Investors

It's interesting to me that there are hundreds of videos on YouTube and commercials on TV that talk about investing in real estate. Everyone talks about investing in real estate. By investing, I'm referring to the commercials for all of those seminars that teach you "<u>How To Buy Real Estate With No Money.</u>" If you've ever turned on the local news channel on a Saturday morning, you've probably seen one of these, so many people get confused when it comes to investing, and they think they need a real estate license.

I want to make sure you understand what the differences are between a Realtor, or agent, and an investor because there seems to be a little confusion. This may be the chapter that causes you to make the decision to go one way or another when it comes to your real estate career.

We've already established that there are many different ways to make money in the real estate business, and I actually teach agents a lot of the ways that they can make money in the real estate business, but for this specific chapter, I'm just talking about being a real estate agent verses being an investor in real estate.

I want to start by talking about investors because, as I mentioned, there's a lot of chatter about investing and how to become an investor or how to invest.

Let's start with investing. I have worked with a lot of investors, and I continue to work with investors today. They tend to be very easy to work with. Investors pretty much are people who put up money themselves, to purchase a property. They're ultimately buying it with the intent of not living in it, but to make some type of profit from it.

We tend to see different types of investors. As referenced in the previous chapters, we have commercial investors and developers. Commercial investors invest in big projects, such as apartment complexes, strip malls, office buildings, etc.

The types of investors that you probably see a lot more of are going to be your flippers and rehabbers. What a flipper or rehabber does is purchase a home for lower than the market value, fix it up, and then resell it for more than they paid for it. That's what's known as flipping a home.

There are also investors who will purchase the property and hold onto it, meaning they don't turn right around and resell it. These investors purchase the property then rent it out. With the acquisition, they purchase the property, get some work done to it if needed, and then they will rent it out for a certain time period. These investors tend to hold onto a property for a longer time than just a flipper. They can hold onto it for years. Their ultimate goal is to generate a monthly rental income.

One other type of investor I want to bring to your attention is a wholesaler. Wholesale investors are pretty much the middlemen if investment deals. They get a property under contract, and while that property is under contract, they sell it to another buyer for higher than they're under contract for. What a wholesaler will get at the closing of the property is the difference between what they have the property under contract for and what they're selling it for. Both closings are happening at the same time. We like to call that a double-close or a simultaneous close. The investor is closing on it with the seller while, at the same time, they're closing on it with another buyer. The profit margins in that area of investing aren't as large most of the time. It all just depends on how low the investor is able to get the property for and how high they can sell it for. There's definitely room for a few thousand dollars profit by doing this.

The real challenge with wholesalers is finding the property and finding the buyer. Keep in mind, these are not real estate agents, so they're not putting the home on MLS, but sometimes they do try to rely on real estate agents to bring them properties to wholesale.

The thing with investing is, if you want to become an investor, you want to have some type of money bank, whether that's a hard money lender, your personal savings, or even a bank that's going to work with you on this. You need to have some type of financial backing. I know that there are "*courses*" and "*trainers*" out there that teach you how to buy properties with no cash and no money down, but my advice, buyer beware.

Personally, I don't work with those types of clients too often. There are tons of creative ways to finance a home, but just be mindful of the person who is trying to make the purchase. The best way for anyone to become an investor is to have cash in the bank that can be used to purchase the property or have a really good lender on your side. I try to tell people all the time, *"Don't feed into the games and gimmicks of the get rich quick schemes."*

Now, let's switch gears and bring it home. As a real estate agent, I'm the person that helps investors, buyers, and sellers. Whatever side the client is on, whether it be investing, or purchasing a primary or second residence, I'm the one that helps them. As an agent, I actively go out, and I find sellers who want to sell their home and move somewhere else or simply just want to get out of it. I put their homes on the market and market them for sale, and I try to find a buyer for them. If the property is appropriate, I'm able to call one of my investor contacts and get the home sold almost immediately.

I'm also the guy who helps the buyers find a home. I do have investments, but I actually chose to go the real estate agent route and work more with consumers because that's what a real estate agent does. As you've probably picked up on by now, a real estate agent can help investors because most times investors need deals. They want to know properties that are coming on the market even before they get on the market. They want to know where the deals are and what's happening, so investors will call on real estate agents a lot. The way that we get paid, if you don't know this by now, is we get a commission of the actual sales price, just like normal. As agents, we're not getting a profit from wholesale deals. We're not getting the difference that's in the middle. We're just getting a straight commission of the sales price.

Investors and Realtors do work hand in hand. I actually look for investors to get listings from, and I look for investors to represent them as their real estate agent. I have really good relationships with many investors in my market, but they are two separate roles. You can do both if you want to, and as a matter of fact, I know a lot of real estate agents who actually own properties to rent or to use as short-term vacation rentals. To sum it up, that's pretty much the difference with investors. They look for the deals, and they typically are not living in the homes, while the Realtors are helping the investors find the deals and helping facilitate the transaction. I hope this cleared up who and what investors are and what real estate agents or Realtors do alongside them.

The Path to 6 Figures

How long do you think it would take actually make a $100,000 in real estate? Before I got into this business, I thought the only way that I would make $100,000 would be if I earned it from a good paying salaried job. Then I saw other agents around me making that kind of money and suddenly it didn't seem so far out of reach. I know it's a big goal of many people to make that kind of money, so I don't want to give anybody false hope. I want to really break down how long it can take you to make a $100,000 or any six-figure number in real estate.

Nothing about the real estate career is a get rich quick scheme. It's funny that people seem to think that, but honestly, there are no real shortcuts. It's important for me to make sure that I'm setting the right expectations so that you can understand what to expect when you get into the real estate industry, and you start to strive for $100,000.

Personally, I had my first six-figure year when I was probably around two and a half years into the business. It did take me quite some time, and that's simply because I didn't know exactly what to do. I had moved around between different brokerages and did some things that I really didn't need to do because I didn't necessarily know the right way to go about all of this.

The first concept I want you to understand before we get into the meat of this is known as client acquisition. You will soon read a whole chapter on client acquisition and customer lifecycle, but for purposes of this context, we will have it mean *how long it's going to take you to get a client*. There is no way that I could possibly know how big your database is or how many people you've helped, but in real estate, there is oftentimes a little ramp up period to actually getting your first client. As agents, we do things like prospecting, marketing, and advertising amongst other things, but just because you put out a marketing piece today doesn't mean hours later your phone is going to start ringing. It's pretty typical for you to have to make eight, nine, ten phone calls or continuously farming an area before you make contact with potential clients.

Client acquisition time is typically the longest amount of time that an agent will experience when trying to get to the closing table. For client acquisition, it can take, typically, around 60 days. 60 days is the time from when someone first sees an email from you or first receives a call from you to them actually saying, "*Yes, we're ready to start working*." Most people start reaching out to a real estate agent two to three months before they're actually ready to buy or ready to start looking. That's to be expected. A call that you receive today may not be ready to go out for a couple of weeks. They may not even be ready to write a contract for a couple of months. I tell agents this all the time, "*An action that you take today, you can expect the results from that action two to three months down the line, so 60 days from now is going to be that client acquisition time.*"

Secondly, there's going to be the time that's needed to go under contract and then eventually close on a home once you've acquired the client. Here's an example. You're working with a buyer, depending on your actual market, it's probably going to take around 15 days before you get them under contract. If you're showing the buyers properties, you're looking at around two weeks or so before you're getting them under contract, and then once you get them under contract you're looking at 30 to 45 days for a closing. From that client acquisition point to closing, you're looking at around four months or so. Typically, this is going to be a rolling thing, so let's just say I get a client today, then I get another one tomorrow, and then I get another one next week. It's going to be a rolling ongoing thing, but I am still looking at around four months from that first acquisition to getting a check from whatever I'm doing with them.

The next thing that you want to think of is how many transactions it's going to take for you to hit that six-figure mark. I want to use the example of a market that has homes for sale with an average price point of $300,000. In that situation, you're looking at around 11 to 12 transactions for you to reach that $100,000 commission.

Divide $300,000 by 0.03 then divide that number into $100,000

That example was using an average price point of $300,000. If you don't want to do 11 deals in 1 year, then you can always raise your price point. I always recommend you do more deals though because that gives you more people to market to. It also gives you more referral sources. Nonetheless, you can always raise your price point. If you're working with a million-dollar property, you're looking at needing only 4 deals to hit six figures.

You can space that out however you want to, but I would say a general rule of thumb is to make sure that you're consistently closing at least one deal per month at that $300,000 and up price point. If you do that, you're going to be making six figures, and you can say at the end of the year that you brought in over $100,000 based on doing those deals throughout the year. Again, this can happen as quickly as you want, or you can spread it out as long as you want. Either way, it's not really hard to do. I would recommend that you take some time to figure out exactly what you would want to do to make that first hundred thousand dollars.

Depending on how hard you work, it can happen a lot quicker, or it can happen a lot slower. There's going to be several other factors that come into play. People are going to test your experience and your knowledge, and that's to be expected. At the end of the day, you know that from the time you acquire a client to the time that you actually close the deal could be three to four months, and you're going to need a certain number of transactions at a certain price point to reach that $100,000 or more commissioned income in your pocket. Something you can do to make this happen quicker is to hire somebody, or you can work as a team with someone else. When you partner up with another agent, there's two or even three of you. If you hire someone on your personal team, there's more people contributing to helping you get to that six-figure commission than just yourself, which can make the process happen quicker. There's a number of ways to do this but I wanted to at least set out a realistic timeframe for you to make that amount of money.

Part Four

Get Your License

Steps To Become An Agent

Becoming a real estate agent is a series of steps that have been outlined and talked about time and time again, yet everyone still wants to know exactly what needs to be done to get started in real estate as a real estate agent, and it's actually pretty simple. It does not take much time to get started in real estate, but it can feel like a long time. The good thing is, the steps are not hard to follow, and I'm going to give you the exact steps you can take.

I'm doing this in hopes that you can get a better understanding of how it all works. Something to note, these steps may vary by whichever state you're looking to become licensed in because every state has different laws and rules, so be sure to check your local real estate commission website.

What I had to do to get started in real estate was pretty simple. The first thing I had to do was enroll in real estate courses, which were pretty easy to find. You can attend any school that is licensed in your state. You can simply do a general search to find all the real estate schools that are licensed in your area. I would recommend checking out the reviews of the school before deciding on one. If you choose to take your classes online, visit my website for my top recommendations.

I personally enrolled in real estate school and took all of my courses online, but you can take yours in the classroom if you are more comfortable with that. If you are interested in knowing the differences between online and classroom, be sure to keep reading because I have a full chapter about that.

When you finish your courses, you will need to register for the actual state exam. Here in Texas, there was a little bit of a waiting period from when I registered to when I actually got to take my test, so I would recommend registering for your exam right after you pass your final exam in your real estate course.

It is a smart idea to take a cram course or exam prep course right before you take the actual state real estate exam. I chose to do this because I wanted to make sure that everything was fresh in my head for when I took that test, and I will say that test was no joke. It was very tricky, and honestly, I didn't think that I would pass on my first attempt. It's not uncommon for people to take the real estate exam a few times, so don't get discouraged if you do fail your test the first time because they make those tests to be very tricky.

After you pass your test, you must register for your license. There was a little bit of a lag time, and here in Texas, you must get fingerprints and background checks to make sure that everything clears out. Once you're fully licensed, you get to have your license sponsored by a brokerage.

While you're waiting for your license to become active, you should take the time to interview with real estate brokers and companies to see where you want to work. Once you choose a broker and get your license, you are full on set to go.

Here in Texas, once licensed and active, you will join our local REALTOR® board and association. Whatever area you're located in, there will be a local REALTOR® association that you can join. There are costs associated with this, so just make sure you get all your details, and be prepared for what you may have to pay.

Wrapping everything up, those are the steps you will need to complete to even get started as a real estate agent. You will need to join a real estate school, pass your state exam, join a brokerage, and finally, join your local REALTOR® association. Once you complete these things, you are ready to sell real estate.

It's that simple.

Online Real Estate Schools

Like we covered in the last chapter, going to real estate school is the first step you need to take to get your real estate license. I repeat - **going to real estate school is the first step that you need to take to get your real estate license**. If you know my story, you know that I've taken real estate classes online, and I've also taken them in the classroom. In this chapter, what I want to do is talk about some of the differences in the different online schools so that you can know what to expect. For me, schooling in the classroom just didn't work out. It's just not for me, but it may be for you. In this chapter I'll be specifically talking about the differences in the online schools.

Let me start by saying that there are a lot of real estate schools that are online and offer real estate courses. When it comes to the actual courses though, they're pretty much all the same as far as course material. The biggest differences with the online real estate schools is the delivery of that material; basically, how it's given to you and presented to you.

The real estate commission in your state decides on the actual curriculum that has to be provided. The actual course content is decided by the real estate commission, which will be a direct reflection of the state exam, and then the school decides how it's delivered to you.

One thing that I was very surprised about though, was that some schools actually just delivered course materials through a PDF textbook. They pretty much just want you to sit there, read the whole textbook, and then they give you exams on it. Who would want to learn that way? They'll give you a final exam, and they'll give you actual lesson exams for the different chapters, but you're literally just reading it from a textbook that they've scanned into a pdf. That's how you're expected to learn.

I couldn't do that. I needed my course to be interactive. If I were just reading hundreds of uninteresting pages from a textbook, I would just fall asleep. That was important in for me in choosing a school.

Another difference that you'll notice between various online schools is their money back guarantees. Surprisingly, some schools don't even offer a money back guarantee. What if, for some reason, you don't like the school? What if you don't like your courses? What if you don't pass your tests? I mean you would want some type of guarantee that you can get your money back, right? These courses are not cheap sometimes, so this was actually another reason why I chose to go to the school that I did. They have a great money back guarantee.

For my online real estate school recommendations, just visit *chastinjmiles.com/school*.

The next thing I want to discuss is the actual course access. You will really appreciate it when your courses are able to be delivered through a variety of mediums. If it's on my cell phone, on my tablet, or on the computer, I should be able to access the course, and it will still be fully functional. Surprisingly though, everyone doesn't have their websites responsive to different platforms like that. I've seen some pretty bad ones. You're literally just downloading, or you're zooming in on a website trying to see it, but it's just counterproductive.

Have you ever read an article on a website from your phone, but the website didn't automatically adjust to your mobile device? Then you've got to zoom in and scroll all over the place to actually read the article. It's almost like you're playing a game or something. Could you imagine taking a whole real estate course on a platform like that? I think not.

Something that really stands out to me is when a school has live instructors. Live instructors are great because if you have a question, they actually have an instructor that you can call, or you can send a message to ask. You can ask questions directly related to the content, or you can simply ask questions just about the school. I really appreciated that because it was really something that blended the whole classroom and online thing. I still felt like I had someone there for me in case I did have a question. I didn't really see a lot of online schools that had that. I don't think I even asked my instructor a question, but just knowing that someone was there, it was very reassuring.

Those were the big differences that I found in the online real estate schools, aside from prices. I did a lot of research before I spent my money because at that point in my life, I didn't have a lot of money, so I used research and reviews to make my choice, which I was very happy with.

Taking The Real Estate Exam

I became licensed here in Texas back in 2013, and I will never forget that real estate license exam. Back in grade school, I was never really a big test taker. I just was never good at tests, and I realized when I took my real estate exam, nothing had changed. That test was extremely tricky. I'm going to try my best to tell you what I remember from the test and what I would do differently if I had to take it again; in regards to studying and preparation. I'm also going to tell you the things that I did that really helped me with the real estate exam.

Surprisingly, I did end up passing my test on the first try, which was a miracle. I passed that sucker by one question. The minimum passing score was a 75, and I got a 76, but hey, passing is passing, and once you pass, you don't ever have to look back at that score again.

About the test. It was broken up into two parts. There was the state portion, and then there was the national portion. The national portion was pretty standard, straightforward questions. It just consisted of a lot of real estate rules and stuff that was just pretty much common sense across the board. The state portion was filled with things that were specific to the state of Texas.

Let me talk more about the national portion. It was a lot easier to me. There were general principles that you can read about in any real estate study book. Where the national portion got difficult for me was the math. There was a good amount of math questions. I remember there being a lot of questions regarding square footage. It asked how many square feet were in an acre, and it asked you to determine the square footage of certain shapes. I had no clue about any of that. There were easier math questions like calculating commissions that I didn't struggle with too much. Alongside those, the test did have other number questions such as determining cost and value methods that investors use, so be prepared to know that type of stuff as well. Another thing that stumped me were questions on things like depreciation of land. To this day, I have a hard time feeling certain about my calculations of those assets.

To be honest with you, math was never my strongest subject, so I didn't go into the math questions super confident from the start.

On the state portion, there was a crap ton of questions about state laws and rules that are pertinent to Texas. I would say around 90% of the questions on my state exam were related to laws. They like to make sure you know the law because there are some things here in Texas that are different from other states. They really ask you those questions to make sure you can distinguish what is specific to this state versus everywhere else. It gets really tricky because they still bring up items that are relevant in other states, so you must know both.

Towards the end of the test, there were questions regarding the Texas Real Estate Commission or TREC. TREC is the actual governing board for the real estate agents. Anything regarding punishment, fines, or breaking laws gets handled by them. They really want you to know specifically what will happen if you do break some rules or break the law. They were a few questions related to ethics.

There were procedure questions, and there were questions about brokerage rules.

Overall, the biggest thing that I took away was that those questions were so tricky. I know I've said that a few times, and I want to tell you what I mean. Tricky to the point where they would give you multiple choice questions, and the answers would have very slight differences in them. For instance, if it was a math question, they may put the decimal in different places in all four of the answers, or they may add more zeros to the numbers, so you've really got to make sure your math is right and tight in order to choose the correct one. They would even ask you questions and provide choices that sounded right, but they weren't. For instance, we were talking about a punishment for breaking a rule. It would say, "*If you do X, what is the punishment? Are you going to be suspended for six months, or your license revoked for six months, or inactive for six months, or on probation for six months*?" You really had to know specifically what would happen if you broke a rule, and unfortunately during my test, they all sounded right to me.

If I had to take it again, the biggest thing that I would worry about is tightening up on my basic math skills. I would study things like how to convert numbers to percentages, where decimals go, and order of operations. I would study how to determine when you need to multiply or divide based on the answer that you're trying to get. That was stuff from high school and college that you just kind of forget as time passes, but it really makes a difference.

I would have also tightened up on my vocabulary. If there's a word that you really don't know, you really want to learn it. Don't just learn the definition, but know when to use it, how to use it, and know the differences in other words that they may be grouped with. That test got so specific. It was crazy.

One of the things that really helped me was taking an exam prep course also known as a cram course. A cram course is literally a quick course that goes over everything that you learned in your real estate course, in a two-day timeframe. I recommend taking a cram course no more than two days to one week before you're scheduled to take the actual test. Even though I did take my classes online, I took a cram course online, and I also did one in person at a local real estate school here in Dallas.

Something else that I did was I created flashcards, which I know sounds basic, but they really helped. There were so many new words to remember, and I was willing to try anything. The flashcards truly helped with the vocabulary.

The last thing I did was go to the bookstore and bought one of those, *Real Estate Exam for Dummies* books. You know, the big yellow ones? I figured it couldn't hurt, and surprisingly, that really helped me with the national portion. I'm guessing that book is sold everywhere, so it has to be pretty general. A lot of things that were in that book were on the national portion of the test, and so it really helped me out.

Looking back, I don't think there's a way to be 100% ready for the real estate exam. I recommend that when you finish your course, you go ahead and schedule your state test. Schedule it for a week out and use that time in between, from when you finish your course to taking the test, to really study hard. Don't forget to take that cram course to really pack it all in. If you wait too late, or if you schedule your test too far out, you're going to start to forget stuff and become overloaded, then it'll just turn into a disaster.

I also want to say, DO NOT be discouraged if you fail on the first try. I have many friends who didn't pass on the first try. It's very common, and I didn't even think I passed on the first try. I remember there was a point when I was taking the test when I just knew I had already failed this, so I was literally clicking answers that just sounded halfway right. I didn't even check my work. It was kind of like I gave up because I just knew I had failed the test.

If you do fail, you can always retake it. It's not a big deal. As a matter of fact, something good could come out of failure because at least you'll know what to expect the next time you take it. If you go back to take it again, it won't be the exact same test. They will jumble up the questions and the answers. You're going to have different questions than the person sitting next to you, which are different from the person's questions across the room.

Also, there's no real way to cheat on this test. These testing agencies are watching you like a hawk. I mean, they have cameras on you, and they're watching your computers. It's a pretty big deal. Try to go into it feeling as prepared as you can, and again, if you fail, you can always go and take it again.

It's not a big deal.

Part 4
Get Your License

Choosing The BEST Brokerage

All active real estate licensees need to have a broker sponsor them. It's very important that you choose the right broker and pick one that is going to help grow your career instead of just letting you hang your license there. Something I recommend you look for is a broker that's selling the type of real estate you want to sell. Whether it's investment properties, apartment locating, or even luxury properties that you're interested in, look for a broker that specializes in that style of real estate. That way you can make sure that all the knowledge, tools, and resources that you need to help your real estate career are right at your fingertips.

Secondly, if you're just doing normal residential real estate, I would search for or seek out a broker that has a strong presence in the geographical area that you are wanting to work in. This was a costly mistake that I made in the beginning of my career. I just went with a big broker because I thought that's what I was supposed to do, but what I learned is that not all brokers have a strong presence in certain areas.

The way you can find out who has a strong presence is by simply driving around. When you're driving around, look and see what company you see more signs for. Call the agents, talk to them, and ask them how real estate is sold at their company. That way, when you're out there pitching yourself to potential clients for your real estate services, they'll at least already be familiar with your firm name.

Something that I would watch out for is brokers promising the world. Most brokers say that they'll do this and that, and when you join on, they're not necessarily doing all those things. Real estate is a business that is oftentimes 100% commission, so you need to be able to generate your own business. Don't fall for the broker that tells you, *"Oh, I'm going to give you so much business, and I'm going to give you so many leads,"* because honestly, it just doesn't work like that. If you find a place where it does work like that, be prepared to pay a price for it.

That brings me to my next point. Try to stay away from those brokers that are going to charge you a lot of ridiculous fees. I'm talking about those brokers who just have charges all over the place. There are brokers out here that just charge a monthly fee that you need to pay to the office, which I can understand. These are called office dues. On the other hand, there are the money hungry brokerages. They charge you for anything possible. They'll charge for copies, faxes, phone usage, long distance calls, signs, and so on.

Then there's those companies that want you to attend programs and trainings to "build your business," but they have a hefty cost. You don't want to go broke before you even get your first transaction going. Look for a broker that can seriously help you out in the business without robbing you.

Choose a broker with great training. Specifically, ask about their training programs. One thing I know a lot of people look for is a mentorship program. If you're going to look for that, make sure it's somebody who can actually mentor you; somebody that you would make a good connection with, and somebody that's not too busy. The way mentorship programs work is, you're being mentored by another agent, and they may get a percentage of your closed deals. When choosing a mentor, don't just try to seek out the top agent in the office. They may be too busy in their business to actually help you and mentor you. If that's the case, don't take that as a sign of rudeness or lack or desire to help. It's just a hefty task to mentor another agent, especially a brand-new agent. There are also mentors that you can find outside of your office. I personally mentor agents all across the country. We do everything remotely, and it works out great. Technology provides so many ways to learn, and you can take advantage of them.

Interview Questions For Brokerages

If you're a new agent, this is probably going to be a completely brand-new experience, especially going into a real estate office and interviewing. Being new to interviewing can be really intimidating. I'm going to explain all of that.

I'm going to give you five questions that you need to ask during any broker interview and the reasons why.

Typically, in a brokerage interview, it's not just a one-way interview in which they are interviewing you to be on their roster. You are also interviewing them to make sure that it's the right place for you. Whenever you go on a job interview, I'm sure there's a million thoughts that go through your head. Luckily, real estate brokerage interviews are a lot less intimidating than an interview at a private law firm. It's kind of a two-way street. They're going to ask you questions, and you have the right to ask them questions. This is pretty common on any type of job interview. It's really just about finding out if it's a good fit for the broker, and if it's a good fit for you.

These questions that I'm going to be giving you are not in any particular order of importance or anything like that. They are just five questions that I feel like need to be asked.

I'm not going to go over the basic questions that a lot of people ask such as, *"Do you all offer leads?"* or *"What's the commission splits?"* None of that stuff. These are more high-level questions that, when asked, will make the broker look at you a little bit differently, in a good way, because you were really thinking about this intelligently.

My first question would be **What is the company culture like**? This is super important. What this is going to do is let you know if the company culture even aligns with what you stand for or how you are as a person in general. Is it a kind of close-knit family environment, or is it just everybody doing their own thing? Do agents see each other regularly? Do they participate in events together? Do they donate to charities together?

All of those questions can help you understand what the culture is like. The environment is created by the culture. You can ask yourself the questions like, "Am I going to feel happy walking in here?" or "Is it just serious and stuffy?" You want to know that because you want to know if you're going to be comfortable working there. You want to align yourself with a culture that really supports you and makes you feel comfortable.

My next question would be **How many agents do you currently have?** Don't take this example I'm about to tell you in a bad way or anything. The first brokerage I joined when I got my real estate license, had like 300 something agents at that one particular office. When I heard that, I thought 300 agents was a good thing. I'm not saying that it's a bad thing, but at the time, I saw 300 agents and thought this brokerage was the place to be. If you have a firm with over 300 agents, then that lets you know that people like working there, and it's very attractive for an agent to work there. The fact that a firm is able to maintain 300 agents shows that they have all the systems in place to train, market, and to help out and provide support to all those agents. Now, if they tell you that there's only 20 agents there, it doesn't necessarily mean anything is wrong, but you may want to consider the reason. Are they a new firm, or are they just more exclusive? It could be possible that nobody wants to work there for some reason or another. You want to find out how many agents currently work there, so that you can know how you're going to fit in.

Sometimes, when it's a super busy office, and there's a lot of agents without a lot of staff to support them, you could get drowned out in the crowd. That's something to think about, but on the other hand, like I mentioned before, the fact that a firm can have a lot of agents can be really good for your career. Use your best judgement when deciding if it's a fit based on the number of agents.

The next question that I would ask or that I would recommend you ask is **How does the brokerage market to bring in business?** This is a big thing because real estate is super stimulated by the community and who knows you. Whose signs do we see and what are they doing within in the community? You want to know from an agent's standpoint what the brokerage is doing to actually market the firm and to market you as an agent. Ask if it's just about the broker, or is it about the actual agents? Is it just about marketing luxury homes or do they market many different types of homes? How can this brokerage help me get sales? That's super important because a lot of brokerages I know still offer things like phone time. Phone time is basically where you could sit at the front desk and answer the phones. If anyone calls, including potential leads, they're yours for the taking. But nobody's going to call if the brokerage isn't marketing itself or its agents. If you're considering a broker that doesn't market out in the community in general, that just means you need to have a really good marketing plan to market yourself.

Next, **How many listings does the brokerage currently have?** This is another thing that can bring in business. The more signs that the public sees with a certain broker, the better it can be for business. When the consumers see specific brokerage signs, it tells them that the brokerage is active in the area and they maintain a lot of listings. It can also make one think that they do a lot of business. Another reason you want to know how many listings the brokerage currently has is that this is also a great opportunity for open houses. What you want to find out is; if you, as an agent, are able to market other listings or possibly hold open houses for some of the listings. Of course, you would have to contact the other agents or the broker and go through that whole process, but brokers that keep a healthy number of listings just really gives you better marketing opportunities.

Lastly, a question that I think is super important to ask is **What's the 5 to 10-year goal or plan for the brokerage?** You want to know where this brokerage is heading. You want to know what things they plan on doing, how big they plan on getting and so on. You want to know what direction they are planning on going in the future. Could they possibly be moving offices? Could they be opening other locations possibly in your town or in another state? When you know the 5 to 10-year goals of a firm, you can be prepared for what's to come. It can give you something exciting to look forward to or it can be something that makes you nervous.

It's possible you may encounter a brokerage that simply says, "*We've done all we want to do, and it's just up to us as agents to work.*" Take that as a red flag. Five to 10 years is a good amount of time for many things to happen. At the 5-year mark, you probably have an image in your head of the agent that you want to be at that time. Does that image line-up with where the brokerage is heading? If not, it may not be the place for you.

The Free Leads Mousetrap

I remember one day I was getting prepared to go and visit with brokers to interview at their brokerages, and to figure out where I wanted to hang my license. I began surfing the Internet looking at blog posts and trying to find videos to see how brokers' interviews go and what questions to ask. I would come across these long lists of questions, and on every single list I would see the question, *Do you all give leads?* I remember going into all of my interviews when I was trying to find my first broker and I specifically asked them, *"Do you all give leads?"*

And they all said, *"YES!"*

You're going to hear yes from a lot of people, but I want to tell you what the truth really is behind that because I was naïve, and I fell for the games.

I just want to tell you right now, it's not what you think it is, and I'm just going to be just brutally honest with you. This whole book I've been telling you about my personal experiences. I've interviewed at a large variety of brokerages when I first got into real estate. I interviewed at all of the big national firms as well as a few local boutique firms. At each interview, I was definitely that agent asking for leads. I also went even further and asked *"So how does your mentorship programs work in conjunction with the leads?"* and then there was *"Will you all supply me with business?"* I clearly remember asking that question over and over again, and I clearly remember all of these brokers telling me, *"Yes, yes, yes, yes we do."* I probably had a couple of them tell me *no*, but for the most part they all told me yes.

I finally signed with a firm that I felt super confident about. What they told me in that interview was pretty much word for word what I read from the articles. I figured this was the one. I remember going in to the office early on my first day because I was so excited, and I just knew that my business was going to take off. I just knew that I was going to be getting all these leads. I was going to be the superstar agent with minimal effort. BEST CAREER EVER!

When I got in there, month one passed, month two passed, month three passed, and surprisingly, I had no leads. I didn't know what was going on. It was almost the opposite of what I was told.

They got me.

Now that I've reflected on it, I realize that nobody gives you leads, and everything that they were telling me was really just to get me in the door and to get me to sign on the dotted line.

Being a more experienced agent now and having seen many things in my career, I'm going to tell you how getting leads works. I know I just said that nobody gives you leads, but I didn't really mean that. I meant that they don't really give you leads the way you think that you'd get them.

First, let's discuss what a lead is. A lead is not guaranteed business, so no matter what you may be thinking right now, just because somebody gives you a lead, it does not equate to dollars in your pocket. That's the first thing you need to get in your head. If I was to send you a lead right now, I have no way to guarantee you that the lead is even going to do anything. At a brokerage level, most brokerages do generate a good amount of leads, and they do have leads coming in from all different sources, but these leads are known for the most part as cold leads. A cold lead means they have no attachment or commitment. They may not even give a correct phone number or a correct email address. You don't know who they are or what they want. The broker doesn't know what they are, and nobody knows what they are until you work the leads and make something out of them.

If it was truly a serious lead, why would a broker give it to you? Especially as a new agent? Why? I apologize, I didn't mean to be so blunt with that, but I had to take note of the elephant in the room.

Just Why? I mean they can obviously give that lead to someone who they know has the systems to work the lead. They can give it to an agent they know has a proven track record of closing deals. Someone they know that has the experience and won't mess up. What incentive does a broker have to give you the good leads? They don't really have any incentive, and that's the first thing that I want agents to understand. Most of the time, if a broker hands you a lead, especially if you're new in your career, they're giving it to you to make you happy and just to follow up on the *YES* they gave you in the interview.

If they had a client that called the office and said, *"Hey, I want to sell my million-dollar home. I need you to send an agent over to my home right now. I want to meet with them today and put it on the market,"* you're probably not going to be the agent to get that lead. However, if one comes in through some random internet form with a very low budget and a few words spelled wrong, they'll probably pass it over to you and hope that maybe it'll turn out to be something. For the most part, they're probably not expecting it to turn into anything significant.

There is a good side to all of this, though. There are upstanding brokers out there who do honestly provide good leads. I have experienced this a few times. With this type of situation, it's common to see them charge you for the lead in some way or another.

Let's just say a broker gives you a lead from their email, or they give you a referral. They may propose that instead of your normal 100% split or your normal 80/20 split, this is going be on a 50/50 split. If a broker does that, I take them, and the lead, a lot more seriously. I will take someone a lot more seriously if they have some type of adjusted split when they give me a lead because then I know they're telling me, this isn't a free for all. *"I want you to work for this. This came in to me, but I'm passing it to you, but I want a bigger cut."* It's totally understandable, and I get it. It's why those are the ones that I'll take a little bit more seriously.

Now, there are brokers out there that'll let you subscribe to lead services, and you can pay a certain amount of money each month. In return, they'll feed you leads through whatever their system is. For the most part, it will probably be a round robin type of thing. You're not going to be the only agent that's a part of the service. As leads come in, they're just going to rotate to other agents depending on the criteria. That's something you can expect from some brokerages, which isn't a bad situation. Keep in mind though, these are mostly internet leads, so they can be very cold and need a lot of work.

I want to tell you, if you're really looking to get some true business from the brokerage, or a broker, or your office, you must have some skin in the game. You've got to show up. You've got to be proving to them, through everything you do, that you want this, and you want to make it happen.

It's a must. You must put yourself out there. I want to say, probably one of the better situations that you can put yourself in if you feel like you need to be fed leads when you get into the real estate business, is going to be joining a team. Team leaders really rely on leads coming in, and they rely on sending those leads to the people that are on their team to get those deals closed. That's their bread and butter. Whatever I do, including all of my marketing I pay for, all the services and subscriptions for lead sources, and all of my mailings, are done to bring in leads to my team. Those leads that come in, I feed out to my team. I want them to actually close, so I'm not just giving those leads out to untrained agents. The people on my team are trained to know how to handle them. There are trained in follow-up. They're trained in overcoming objections. They are ready to go. Whenever a lead is sent to their email, they call and email them immediately when they come in, and that's the way that it should be.

There are ways to get good leads in real estate, but I'm going to tell you: Don't just believe all the hype about getting in leads from a broker because it's not necessarily what you think it is. Keep in mind, this isn't for every type of situation. This isn't 100% of the time, but I will say this is a majority of the time, so you just have to be mindful of the fact that you are a new agent, and you don't have much experience.

You don't have much skin in the game yet.

You're going to want to be able to get with somebody and align yourself with someone that can help you build your real estate career, and there's so much more in building this real estate career than just feeding you leads. Leads costs money, especially the good ones. Since they cost money, consider if your broker is going to want to give it to someone who is experienced. Is that firm really invested in you? Do they want to just add you on a roster, or do they want to keep you on the roster?

Groups and Teams

The name of my real estate team is Founders Real Estate Group. Before Founders, my team was named The Chastin J. Miles Real Estate Team. It got to a point one day that I decided that I didn't want it to all be about me. Then it was renamed the CJM team; everything was branded and marketed around Chastin. This left little room for the actual agents on the team. Sure, I put the team together, but we were all smart and hard-working individuals but it left little room for everyone else. So today, we are known as The Founders Group. That's just a bit of history on my team journey. I seem to have gotten ahead of myself. Let me backtrack a little bit and give you some real information about teams.

A team is an organization within a brokerage that branches off and does their own thing. It's normally run by a team leader or maybe two leaders who are top producers in their market, and they get together to expand their businesses. Within a team structure, it's pretty common to see a lead agent or the team leader, and then they'll have buyer's agents, seller's agents, and then sometimes they'll even have a transaction coordinator, a marketing person, and an administrative assistant to do all of the backend work. Here's what you can expect by actually joining a real estate team.

Most teams are all about the team leaders. One thing you will notice is that everything falls under the team's name and brand. This sometimes doesn't work too well for someone looking to be that individual superstar agent because you probably won't get that by joining a team. You're working under someone who had already made it and already has a brand name built for themselves. You're going to be lifting the whole team name instead of your individual personal name and brand.

When you do join a real estate team, the other members and leaders are going to expect you to work really hard. You're going to have someone, if not many people, holding you accountable and you're going to have goals that you will need to meet. They're not just going let you come in and run with the team name and not do anything. There's actually a higher level of accountability in a real estate team than you would experience as an individual agent. Just know that.

One of the reasons I actually encourage new agents to join teams is that there is a quicker startup period. You're essentially taking yourself, with no real estate experience or many transactions, and placing yourself in the team environment where there's most likely leads coming in and deals happening all the time. You're going to get educated quickly, and you're going to get to work pretty quickly.

That brings me to my next point. You're most likely going to get a different level of training on the team. When you step into a team environment, you're going to do things the way that the team is accustomed to doing them. You're going to do things the way that your team leader has set forth. Keep in mind, they know what works. Don't be surprised if they do things slightly differently than the actual brokerage they belong to. Just be prepared to follow the flow of the team.

One last thing that you may notice is that, on a team, you will have a different split than your current brokerage or the company. Since you are on a team, a team is going to have a split of its own, on top of your actual split that you have with your brokerage. There's most likely going to be a team split under that. Something I like to tell people is that if you're a new agent, even joining onto a team, you're going to make money quicker. It may be more frequent because the team oftentimes has a full pipeline of people ready to go. They may have systems set in place in which you can really make a difference and grind hard to get make money more quickly. This can really help out a struggling agent like I once was. I simply did not even knew teams even existed so I left myself little room to even seek one out.

Part 4
Get Your License

Understanding Splits A Bit Better

You know, before I got into real estate, I had the hardest time calculating how broker splits worked. I know I already told you that I wasn't good at math, and I just couldn't figure out this whole split thing. When I was interviewing with various places, I would hear people say 70/30, 50/50, 60/40, but I literally had no clue what they were talking about. I just knew in my head that you wanted to go for the higher number, I guess, but I didn't know which was the higher number I was looking for. It was just a big mess. I know I'm not the only one out there that has had this difficulty. Maybe you're experiencing this right now. So, I want to tell you how brokers splits work and how you can calculate them in hopes that you will know how to calculate your commissions in the future.

Brokers oftentimes charge some sort of split because it's how they make their money. The split can be very high, or it can be very low. It can pretty much be anything. It can be whatever the broker gives you, so the best way to understand how splits work is to think about an example of me giving you $1. With this $1, I want you to give half of it to your friend, and you can keep the rest. That's pretty much *the split*. Basically, I'm telling you to split the money between your friend and yourself. That's the basic rule behind a split. Now to make this more realistic, let's use some real numbers. For this example, we will use a 70/30 split. Basically, that's the broker deciding how much money you get and how much they're going to keep from each one of your real estate transactions.

The same goes for 50/50. The broker is saying I'm keeping 50 percent and you get to keep the other 50 percent. An easy reference for this is knowing the first number is going to be the number or percentage that the agent will get. The second number is going to be the percentage that the broker gets, so with that 70/30 you're going to get 70 percent of the dollar amount and the broker's going to get 30 percent of the dollar amount. For a 50/50 split, you get 50 percent, and the broker gets 50 percent.

Now, onto the real numbers. Let's use the example of a $500,000 home. On a $500,000 home, you earn the standard three percent commission, so you will bring three percent into the brokerage. That's going to come out to $15,000. Based on the amount of $15,000, you will calculate your split. If you're getting a 70/30 split, then on that $15,000, you're going to take home $10,500. If you're on a 50/50 split, you're going to take home $7,500 because half of that is going to the broker, and half of it is going to you. With that example, you are simply multiplying the total commission by your split percentage. Use that first number, the 70% or the 50% or the 60%, whatever your number is.

Keep in mind, depending on your brokerage, you may have more fees on top of that. Some brokers charge franchise fees, or they may charge you for E&O insurance on each one of your transactions. Some may even have transaction fees. It's important for you to read your paperwork and talk about this in your initial meetings with your broker to find out if there are fees on top of your split.

A lot of agents think that those fees are just built into the split until they get their final closing statements, and they're wondering where all these other fees are coming from, so check with your broker.

Now, here's a little secret when it comes to splits, and most agents don't know this, but most of the time, splits are negotiable. Some brokerages do have different split structures such as tiered splits. These splits depend on how much you sell. Your split gets higher the more real estate you sell, and you can eventually cap out at a certain amount.

Before you try to negotiate a split, make sure you have some valid leverage points. If you're a brand-new agent, no experience, you're going to need a lot of training. The broker is going to have to put a lot of time and effort into you. If that's your situation, you don't need to walk in trying to get the highest split. Think of a split like an investment. You're going to be investing in the broker and into the brokerage name, the training, and everything that comes along with it. Now, if you are a seasoned agent or you have some transactions under your belt, and you're bringing something to the table, then yeah, I would say sit in the interview, negotiate a good split for yourself, something that you're comfortable with, and something that the broker is comfortable with. People do it all the time; it isn't uncommon, but a lot of people just don't know that you can do this. Even if you are brand new, it never hurts to try.

The broker is most likely going to give you the lower number to start out with, and if that doesn't work for you, then try to raise it up a bit, but just make sure it makes sense. There are 100% brokerages out there. There are all kinds of different splits around this industry. My advice is don't just look for the biggest number. I learned that the hard way. Really evaluate what you're getting and if it makes sense for you to pay into the brokerage what you're paying per transaction.

Part Five
Understanding The Business

The Customer For-Lifecycle

Not everything is just about real estate itself, but also about dealing with clients. The customer lifecycle is something that I practice in my business daily, and I've been perfecting it for many years. There are things within it that you're going to pick up on and know how to do, but it's really letting this process internalize so that you know how to conduct you business the best way when dealing with clients.

Most agents simply focus all their time on getting clients, but keeping clients is where the money lies. It's important that you keep clients for the future, so I want to show you the life cycle of the clients that you're going to get. That way you can have business for many years to come.

You probably hear from a lot of real estate agents who have been in the business for a while that they get a lot of business from referrals, and this is exactly how that happens. If you begin to practice this, as you start to do transactions and as your business grows, you'll be getting in those referrals along the way. When we refer to my client life cycle, just keep that in mind, this is the process for you to not only get business, but for you keep business coming in. It's super important.

When it comes to the customer life cycle, I like to break it up into a little acronym known as **A**, **P** and **R** and no, we're not talking about interest rates. I'm going to go through each of these for you so that you can understand them. I'm also going to tell you what takes place in each of these stages in your business so that you can pretty much apply all the practices to it.

We start with **A**. This is our first step every time, it's whats known as our **acquisition phase**. This is the phase you're going to go through with acquiring clients. The process of getting business occurs in the acquisition phase. We have four different areas: marketing, leads, qualify, and nurture. Each step follows the previous step.

As an agent, you're going to market for business. You should be doing whatever you need to do to market, whether it's placing ads somewhere on social media or sending out postcards. Whatever way you choose to market, do it well. That's going to be the absolute first step. From your marketing, you're going to start getting leads. When those leads come in, it's going to be important for you to qualify those leads. Are they qualified to purchase? Are they qualified to rent? When are they looking to purchase? When are they looking to sell? Whatever the case may be, you're going to qualify them with whatever your process is. Qualifying the lead will give you a clear indication of whether they are serious or not and how much time you should invest into them.

Next, comes the nurturing phase. Not everybody is going to be ready to go immediately when they call you, and sometimes people need to be nurtured to get warmed up to you and figure out if they really want to do business with you. During this nurturing phase, you are following up with them, keeping yourself on their radar. Possibly provide any ideas or quick solutions to any problems they may have or any hesitations. They should be on your email drip campaign, as well as on your call and text follow-up campaigns.

After the acquisition phase, is the **P** which stands for the **performance phase.** This is the time for you to shine. This is the time that you put on that real estate agent hat, and you actually do what needs to be done to get the client. In this performance phase, the steps are appointment, give value, get agreements signed, and then do the job.

Let's discuss the appointment. After you've nurtured them, they're ready to meet, whether it's a listing appointment or a buyer's consultation. You're going up to that appointment step. Once you get in the appointment, you must absolutely give as much value as possible. Your value is going to tell them why they should hire you. You're going to tell them everything that you need to tell them so that they can make an informed decision when it comes to hiring you as their agent. You can only do that by giving value, not just talking about yourself. It needs to be valuable to them.

Once they've decided that they want to hire you, get your agreements signed. Don't do anything without getting your agreements signed. Get your agreements signed immediately when they agree to work with you.

Once that's complete, you're going to actually do the job; you're going to perform. Performing means listing the home or going out to help them buy; you're going to do the actual job you've been hired for. By doing the job, I'm talking about everything from showing the properties to closing. All that stuff is part of the job, so you're going to do all of that during this performance stage. That's why I like to call this performance because you're performing.

Lastly, this is where the **R** comes in. This is known as the **retention phase** where you're going to retain them as clients. Have you ever heard somebody say that they want to create a customer for life or have a client for life? This is what happens during this stage. By your actions, you're retaining them as a client. The items in the retention phase happen post-closing; after you've gotten paid and they've moved in. If you haven't made it to closing yet, you're still in one of the previous phases. Before you get to where you're retaining them, you need to make sure that you get all the way to completion in the performance phase.

These are things that I do in my business during the retention phase. The biggest thing that you're going to notice when you're doing these actions is that this is what's going to bring in the referrals. You can do a good job as an agent, and you may get an immediate referral, but by doing these four things that I'm about to lay out, you're going to really start to see an increase and a steady flow of referrals.

The first thing that I do is send out monthly newsletters through email. They get a newsletter letting them know what's up with me, my business, and the team. Alongside that, I call them once a month to just check in. I'm not necessarily asking for business or asking for referrals but I'm keeping my name out there by calling once a month. Remember this is a relationship business, so you want to keep that relationship with these people going. I just call, check in with their family, see if they've been on any vacations, and see what they have planned for the near future. It goes along way.

In addition to that, we're sending out quarterly gifts. We're not spending a lot of money on the gifts, but it's just something cute that we send out once a quarter. This is just another way to keep your name in front of them.

Lastly, we have our client appreciation events. These are held twice a year; one in the winter and another one in the spring where we invite all of our past clients out and treat them to drinks and appetizers. We let them network with each other and even play games.

Clients should never tell anyone, "*My agent hasn't contacted me.*" That is a big issue we have in this business right now, and there've been numerous articles written about it. Whenever people are ready to buy and sell again, most times they use a different agent because they lost touch with their previous one. They've either lost the phone number, or they haven't heard from them. Whatever the reason may be, they use a different agent. It's during this phase that you're going to really make sure that it doesn't happen to you.

Again, you're going to start to see a lot of referrals come in just from those simple actions. This is my customer life cycle. You can always remember it. A, P, and R-Acquire, Perform, and Retain. Those are the big three.

Some people get stuck in the acquisition phase and in the nurture stage. A lot of leads fall off during this nurture stage. They don't necessarily move over to the appointment. You can prevent this by using a good and proven process.

Training Your Career Away

There's damn near a training class for just about everything. One can literally go crazy trying to figure out what classes to take, how to get trained, and always feeling like you need training. Let me say this, most agents will never get to the point where they know everything. I don't even know everything myself. I don't know any real estate agent that knows everything, and there will always be opportunities to learn something. On the other hand, I feel like there are some people who just over-exaggerate on these trainings, and it gets them nowhere. They take classes such as *How to Be a Certified Appraiser* and pay $50, only to learn that appraisers exist, and it's their job to appraise properties.

As agents, we just need to sell homes and be real estate agents. Let me just give you the essentials so that you don't fall into this money trap. I'm going to tell you the trainings that you should take that will literally last your whole career. If you want to take other classes and receive designations that guarantee nothing, then that's fine, but these are going to be the ones that you should always seek out and take them when you have an opportunity.

The first training that I always recommend taking is any sort of lead generation training. You won't make any money in this business unless you have leads and business coming in. Therefore, you want to know how to drum up leads. I recommend taking a social media class, or door knocking, cold calling, etc. You just need to know how to drum up leads. A lead generation class is extremely important when it comes to this business and any sales business.

Next, you need to take marketing classes. You want to know how to market yourself and how to market your business. As you start to drum up leads, people are going to start looking you up, and you better hope they like what they see. When you start meeting with both buyers and sellers to do listing presentations, your presentation is key, so you need to know how to market yourself and how to market your business.

Marketing goes far beyond just designs and logos. For me, marketing is a true passion of mine. I've learned that you really want to make sure your marketing is top notch in your business because trust me, people are going to look it up. They're going to look up the reviews; they're going to look you up on Google. They're going to really try to investigate you and try to see who you really are, even before you step into the door. Marketing classes are always great. Plus, the more marketing skills you learn, the less you've got to pay other people for marketing.

The next important thing that you need to know is how to be a sales person. You need to know how to close leads. You need to know how to make a deal happen as you're walking through a home with people from an open house. You need to know the things to point out, and you need to know how to overcome objections.

A real estate agent is a salesperson, and this is where a lot of people fall off in this business because they don't know how to be a salesperson. You can have all the great marketing and all the great lead-generation tactics, but you need to know how to sell. You need to know how to turn that "no" into a "yes," so having a sales background or having sales experience is definitely helpful to a lot of people in this business. If you don't have previous experience, don't worry; there are tons of books out there. There are tons of classes that can teach you how to sell and how to be a closer. I definitely think it's super important for any real estate agent. I'm telling you these in the order that I would recommend you gain knowledge and learn.

Everybody tries to run and learn contracts, documents, procedures, and so on. Something that I always tell people, especially if they belong to a brokerage, is that they're going to make sure that your contracts are good. They're going to make sure that your documents are signed. They're going to make sure that you're doing the right thing when it comes to those things. What people don't realize is that you need to have business to even have a document to fill out. Something that kind of messed me up when I was getting trained and figuring this business out was that I attended all these classes on documents and contracts, and by the time I actually needed to use the information, I had forgotten it. I didn't know how to generate business. I didn't know how to market myself, and I didn't know how to close over the phone or in person, so I didn't have clients.

Believe me, in this business, there are plenty of resources to teach you how to write a contract or to teach you the process of contract to close. There are so many different resources out there, and honestly contracts is the easy part. It's so easy. You can literally open a how-to book, and it will tell you how to go through a transaction.

Other things, that I feel are a lot more important than learning documents, are going to be your market knowledge. You want to be knowledgeable about your market. You can do this very easily. What I would do is I would hop on MLS every day for maybe around 30 minutes to an hour and just see what was new, what had expired, and what had sold. This is something you should be doing anyway. You can take it a step further and actually go out and tour properties. You should go out there and check out anything that's new on the market. If there is an open house or a broker's open, stop by those because you want to be able to speak intelligently to your leads and prospects when they're asking you about different homes in the area. I definitely recommend that. If you're in a big city like I am, it's going to be nearly impossible to know the whole city, so you want to go ahead and focus on the area where you want to work. Granted, you're probably going to work all over the place, but we can all have that one market area that we know like the back of our hand. You need to have one of those areas, and that's where that market knowledge comes into play.

Attend your local MLS meetings, if they have them in your area. The markets change frequently, so if you can get into a habit of keeping up with your market, you will always be one of the most knowledgeable agents around.

You Did What You Said You Would

I got my first listing maybe six or seven months after being licensed in the business. You would have thought I would have closed a deal by then but that wasn't the case. My first listing didn't come until after I had already moved from one real estate firm to another. I was in Dallas, and I needed some business. I needed something. I was broke and I needed something just to help me stay afloat.

I was still in that beginner stage or that new agent stage. Luckily, it was still that stage where I was willing to literally try anything. Whatever I had to do, I was going to do it. I was completely desperate.

I would go into the office every day. As a matter of fact, I was always one of the first people in the office every morning. There was this one guy in the office every morning with me. He would immediately come in, and he would hop straight onto the phone. He would literally cold call people. I had heard of this, but I had never seen it in action. This guy, Chad was his name, would cold call every single day! He was using the same script and was saying the same thing to people every single day. I could hear him loud and clear, as a matter of fact, I practically memorized the script myself simply just from hearing him. I don't know if he got results from it, but I know that he got a lot of people saying "No." I mean, hopefully he did get some listings. I wasn't really able to hear the conversation on the other end of the line, but I admired his persistence. It motivated me to want to try it.

One day, I decided to ask him for his script, and he was actually more than willing to give it to me. I went to the copy machine to make a copy of his script, then I handed it back to him. As I went back to my table I said, "*Okay, well I have nothing to lose.*" At that point, I knew that I was going to try this whole cold calling thing. I'm going to actually try to get a listing with Chad's script. Then, my nerves got the best of me. I chickened out. I didn't start that day.

The next day, I came into the office. Actually, it wasn't even the next day; it was probably like three or four days later, I came in dressed and ready to go. This was round 2. Go time!

I had the script printed out. I was sitting in front of a computer. I didn't have a laptop at the time because I had pawned it for cash. I was using the office computer, and I just sat there. I had all my notebooks, all my notes, and everything. One would have thought I had this all figured out. If I didn't know anything else, I knew that I was prepared, and I was about to hit those phones and make some stuff happen. Once I had everything positioned, I started looking around. I asked myself, *"Who am I going to call?"* I realized, I don't have any phone numbers! I have this script, my notebook, my blank calendar just so I could check my availability for the appointments. But I didn't have phone numbers. How dumb of me. So, I did what any millennial would do, I got on Google and I typed in *"for sale by owners."* Guess what came up? A website that was literally called forsalebyowner.com. I clicked the link only to see that they had listings on there as well as phone numbers to the actual homeowners on this website. It couldn't get any better than this. This is a website where homeowners can go in and place their own properties in hopes of selling them without a real estate agent. I scrolled, scrolled, scrolled, and I said, *"What the hell? Let's just go for it."*

I called one number; they didn't answer. I called another number; they didn't answer. It wasn't until my fifth one that I ended up dialing a guy who answered. The first words out of my mouth were, *"Hello, this is Chastin Miles,"* (no J. at the time) *"with Keller Williams and I'm calling..."*

The guy on the phone stopped me.

He said, *"So you're a real estate agent?"*

My quivering, less-than-confident voice replied, *"Yes sir."*

Then he just starts talking again. He says, *"I'm sure you see my home on a website. What questions do you have?"*

By this time, I diverted back to my script. I ask, *"So, why did you decide to sell your home FSBO?"* and *"Where are you going to go after this?"* I didn't even pay attention to the photos clearly showing me the home was vacant. I was going downhill.

He stops me again and says, *"How much do you think my house is worth?"*

I reply, *"Well, I don't really know yet. I would have to go ahead and run some comps on it, and I can let you know."*

He responds with, *"Okay, run some comps on it and call me back,"* and the call ended.

In my head, I knew it was all over. I got off the phone simply knowing that now it was time for me to figure out how to run comps.

I asked another agent that was in the office to help me run some comps, and luckily, he agreed to help. We did it in about 15 to 20 minutes. After I ran those comps, I called the seller back. I said, *"Sir, based on what we found, the home should be worth around $XXX,XXX."* I don't remember the exact number, but it was in the low two hundred thousand range.

He said, *"Okay,"* and then there was silence. He took a deep breath in and sounded like he was really bothered. I was sweating bullets on the other side of the phone waiting.

I said *"Okay."* I don't know why I said "okay." It was out of pure nervousness.

Then he suddenly says, *"You know, you were the first real estate agent that I ever spoke with, and believe me, I received many calls from this website, but you're the first real estate agent who actually did what they said that they were going to do. You actually called me back with the information that I requested, so I'm going to give you the listing."*

This was the most exciting time in just my whole career. In my head, I was like, *"Oh my gosh, I got a listing, I got a listing!!"*

He proceeds to say, *"Send me whatever you have to send me. I will electronically sign it, and there's already a lockbox on the door. I'll give you access to it."* I knew there had to be a catch, this can't be, is it really this easy? Sure enough, I quickly filled out the listing agreement, with help of course, and I sent it over to him. He electronically signed it and gave me access to the property. That was literally how I got my first listing.

It was so crazy how it all went down. Once he told me that, I couldn't believe it. and I wondered what had I been waiting on this whole time?

It turns out he was an investor. He gave me that listing, and he gave me another one after that. Just from growing some balls and deciding to cold call, I got my first listing. Fast forward cold calling is a daily part of my business. It started with making the decision that I was going to do something out of my comfort zone and following through with it. I didn't know what the result was going to be, but by just following through and doing what I said I would do, I earned me my first piece of business.

The Cost Of Selling A Listing

We've all heard the saying that nothing in life is free, and that's especially true when it comes to real estate. I'm sure you've worked hard to get going in real estate, and I would imagine you really want to make some money. Well, let me tell you, you're going to have to spend some money to make some money. Have you ever been to a casino and played a penny slot? The slot machine just pays you back in pennies. On the other hand, when you play a dollar slot, it pays back in dollars. Real estate is the same concept. The more you put into it, the more you can possibly win from it. In real estate, listings are the name of the game, even though, as a new real estate agent, you'll probably start out with a buyer transaction. Your goal should really be to get listings. When you take on a listing, there are some costs that are pretty much definite that you can expect every time.

The first important cost when you get a listing, even before you go and put it in MLS and on the real estate websites, is to invest in professional photography. Photos make all the difference when it comes to getting attraction. On average, I probably spend around $150 on photos for a home less than 3000 square feet. A larger home will require more expensive photography. The cost of photos is directly determined by the square footage of the home. With larger homes there's more exterior, interior, as well as other features, so just budget accordingly for that. I wouldn't dare present a property without professional photography. Remember, this is a part of your marketing. People will see the photos you put out.

Next, you're going to need marketing materials, also known as marketing collateral. Marketing materials are going to be things like your postcards, flyers, brochures, books, and of all those good things that you're going to use inside and outside of the home to market it. Consumers actually look at these things, and they take them with them. They are going to help sell the listing, of course, but they also help you sell your personal brand. When buyers or sellers see these materials, they're going to know what type of presentation you give in your business. Just think, if a seller comes into a home that you have for sale and sees magnificent marketing materials, they may want to hire you to sell their home.

Moving right along, you are going to need a lockbox for the door and a sign for the yard. Lockboxes and signs are an investment. I'm saying that because they're not cheap. The good thing about lockboxes and signs is that once you make the investment, you can use them over and over again, and you are going to use them over and over again. If you are up for your first listing, be prepared to spend some money on your lockboxes and your signs. Before you make that investment, check with your broker; they may have specific signs that the brokerage uses.

Next, you are going to need to market the property in order to get it sold. To be honest with you, I could write a whole book on this alone. I may consider writing a book on just things that you can do to market a property. This is very important. A few common marketing routes that could cost you are things such as social media advertisements, open houses, videos, events, and magazine and newspaper advertisements. All of these are going to cost some money, and the longer that your home is on the market, it's more than likely you will have to do more and more marketing, so be prepared for these expenses to add up. If it's a luxury property, your seller may want to see things like magazine and newspaper articles, TV features, and more.

Keep in mind, each of these items is relative to the property. Whether it's a $100,000 property or a million-dollar property, it's going to be relative to what you're going to spend and how you market it. You always want to put your best foot forward because you want to make your clients happy.

More importantly, you never know who's watching. You can get another deal from a listing. It happens all the time. You put on a great presentation for one listing, and you're going to have another one waiting for you.

Part 5
Understanding The Business

How To Work With Homebuyers

Knowing how to work with different types of clients is going to help you overcome more in your business and become more successful. By knowing your client, you can overcome objections more easily because you know the things that are important to specific types of clients. Through the years, I have commonly interacted with three different types of clients. I have mastered how to work with each of them, especially when it comes to them buying a property. I have come to know what's really important to each of them, and it ultimately helps me sell more efficiently.

The types of buyers that I encounter are the ones that I want to talk about in this chapter. The types of buyers are:

1. Emotional buyers

2. Practical Buyers

3. Financial Buyers

It's pretty easy to know which buyer you are dealing with, and it's even easier to know how to handle and work with them.

Let's start with emotional buyers. You can often identify emotional buyers right off the bat when you are showing a property to them for the first time. It's kind of crazy because you can't really tell too much until you actually get them in a home, but these are the ones who will walk in the home and automatically use words to describe the home. They will say, *"Oh, this is just beautiful, and I love these windows and I love the floors and oh, everything is just so pretty."* They use words like love and gorgeous. You may even hear them drop the word perfect from time to time. They talk a lot about the aesthetics of the home. They're most likely going to be the buyers that comment about things like furniture, wall colors, flooring, and finishes. They get very emotional about the actual look of the property. With emotional clients, you want to point the things out that you know they will love. Not only do you point them out, but you will also want to make examples using their lifestyle. An example of that would be *"The natural light in this room would be perfect for your craft projects."*

We've all encountered these emotional buyers. If you've ever shown any of them a property, they talk a lot with their feelings. They walk into a room and say, this room makes me *feel* like this, or *I can see* this in this room, or *I can see* that. They're easy to spot, and they tend to be very vocal about how they feel when they're in an actual property. You can look for those things and that'll let you know that you have an emotional buyer.

The next type of buyers are the practical buyers. Practical buyers are the ones who know specifically what they want and the reasons they want them. Those are the ones that are going to point out things like, the size of a room for a growing family. They will also make sure you know that need to be zoned for a specific school or in the vicinity of a certain place. Practical buyers will have a reason for everything, and they will be very vocal about those reasons. They don't make decisions solely on the aesthetics but often try to make sure a property is conducive to their needs in their life. You may hear some of them say, "*I travel a lot, so I need to be close to the airport,* and *I need these types of things in the homes.*" and "*I would prefer a condo with a doorman or with concierge because of these reasons.*" They are forming the property around their lives and the necessities in their lives. Be sure to pay close attention to their specifics because that's what is going to ultimately help you sell to them. They're going to be very practical about their decisions.

When it comes to a specific property, practical buyers aren't the people you want to necessarily point out views or cabinet finishes to. Those things are simply not important to them. Practical buyers really care about their family, their needs, their work, and the functionality of their home. When they are really considering a property, they will often ask themselves, "*Is this home what my family and I need, and is this a home that I will allow us to do XY & Z?*" As a salesperson, you want to be sure that you uncover the things that are truly important to them.

The last type of buyer that I tend to identify are known as financial buyers. Financial buyers are literally purchasing just based on finances alone. A lot of decisions that they make are going to be closely related to money. Their decisions are motivated by money, so they're going to ask a lot of questions pertaining to money. You will commonly hear financial buyers say things like, "*How much do you this would cost to change? How much do you think this would cost to add in? What are the HOA dues here? What do you think this investment would be worth in two, three, five years*?" They're going to ask a lot of money questions. These buyers may stump you, if you aren't prepared for them. A financial buyer will commonly point out a property that may have just sold on the same street and how much it sold for.

Investors are big financial buyers. Investors tend to be more financially motivated, and that's their actual style because they're investing. They are either flipping the properties, renting them out, or they're doing a wholesale deal. When purchasing becomes more of a financial decision rather than an emotional or practical one, you're dealing with a financial buyer. Some financial buyers don't even really even care about the way that the property looks when they first walk in. They don't really care if it'll work for them or not because they will most likely be purchasing it for temporary reasons.

What's most important to a financial buyer is the bottom line numbers. How much is it going to cost them to get into it? How much can they sell it for? How much work do they have to put into it? Those are the things that are going to motivate them. If you find yourself dealing with those types of clients, you need to know your numbers. Some things you can study would be the geographical areas, the costs of materials, what the appreciations are like in the area, and any upcoming news that could affect values in the area. All those things are going to be important to a financial buyer as they make those investment decisions.

Something to watch out for with buyers, especially couples, is that there may be a combination of buyer types. You can tell that one person cares more about the money and the other cares about the practicalities of the property. There are some buyers that throw money at anything, and there are some who want more than they can afford.

The best thing you can do as an agent is to learn to speak to them in their decision language because ultimately, that's going to make you a better agent in their eyes, and it's going to be able to help you get a specific property sold. It comes down to you learning to connect with your clients because, at that point, you can basically take almost any property and sell it to either one of these types of buyers.

Wasting Time With Unreal Buyers

Have you ever experienced a time when you were dealing with a buyer, and you didn't quite know if they were real or if they were wasting your time? It gets to that point when all of those negative thoughts pop into your head. If you haven't yet, be ready. I know I certainly have, so I want to give you some tips on ways to spot fake buyers. I'm calling them fake buyers because they're probably going to be the buyers that end up being a big waste of your time or not the best use of your time at the moment.

Being in the industry for a while, I've been able to work with a lot of different clients, and I've been able to pick up on things that really separate the people who are serious and real versus the people who may just want to look at houses and aren't true real estate buyers at this point.

When I refer to this select group of people as fake buyers, I don't necessarily mean they won't ever buy a house, but I do mean that they're probably not worth your time and efforts right now. These buyers are not worth the time for you to get in the car and show them properties over properties because in the end, you will do all of that and they probably will not be buying a property right now. These are the things that you can look out for and know ahead of time if you should perhaps take a second look at them to determine if they're worth it right now.

The first sign is, and it's pretty obvious, are those buyers who don't want to discuss finances. It's so interesting to me that people will seriously keep the finances a secret when they are purchasing a home. Whether they're purchasing a home with cash or if they're obtaining financing through a mortgage company, we must talk about money because there is a large amount of money involved. Anybody who's trying to hide their money situation is probably not a true buyer at that time.

I've worked with buyers who have a lot of money. I'm talking millions of dollars-worth of cash just sitting in their bank account, and they have no problem talking about it when it's appropriate. I've also worked with people who don't have much money, who are getting a loan, and they have no problem talking about it. It's not about how much money someone has; it's all about the principle. Anyone who comes to you saying they don't want to talk about money or giving vague responses like, "*I have enough*," are buyers that are probably going to be a waste of your time. With those buyers, you want to take a closer look at their overall situation. If someone is seriously considering purchasing a home, they have no problem discussing how they're going to pay for it.

The next red flag I recognize is when I hear people say that they'll buy a property anywhere. The exception to these buyers is going to be investors. Most true homebuyers won't buy a property anywhere. When you've talked to a new lead and you ask them, "*Where would you like your new home to be?*" and they respond with "*It can be here. It can be there. It can be anywhere*," they may just want to look at homes.

I learned this on one of my first buyer experiences. I live in a very large city. Dallas is huge. We're talking miles and miles of real estate. One buyer with whom I was working with didn't have a specific area in mind. The first red flag when dealing with this was that he didn't want to talk about how he was going to pay for the property. Then I noticed, as I was showing him homes, we were traveling to all different parts of the city. We were going into towns and suburbs that were sometimes 20 to 30 miles away from each other. You can probably guess, he didn't end up buying anything. I later found out, he didn't even have a car. It was just a time wasted situation altogether. Serious buyers tend to know where they want to live or at least have a general idea. They may not know a specific subdivision, but they at least have an area lined up because anyone who works, has a family, or does recreational activities in certain areas, is going to know where they want to be. It's never a good idea to work with a buyer with an *I don't care, anything goes, or just show me houses wherever I'm open* attitude.

*Next, t*here are those buyers who aren't willing to follow and respect your process. Everything that I do in my business is a process. I have steps one through 10 already lined out. It's a process. Before I even go and show someone a home, I have certain things that need to happen prior to us getting in the car together or before I unlock a door and enter a property alone with them. It's all a process, and any buyer who's not willing to follow your process is probably not a serious buyer. Let's use the example of visiting the doctor's office. You don't just walk into the doctor's office and go straight to the doctor and say, *"Check me out. Tell me what's wrong with me?"* No. They have a process. You're going to call and make an appointment. Then you're going to show up at your appointment time and probably speak to a receptionist to get signed in. They're going to check your insurance, then instruct you to sit in the waiting area. When they call you back, they'll take your vitals, which include your measurements, weight, height, blood pressure, and so on. The nurse may take a statement of what's going on with you and then the doctor comes in. When the doctor speaks with you, he or she may prescribe you whatever medicine or perform whatever treatment that you need. But it's a process. Everyone running a serious business has a process, even a lawyer. There's a process and that goes the same for real estate. Anybody who's not ready and willing to follow your process is simply a distraction from a serious buyer. Serious buyers have no problem filling out paperwork, scheduling a showing for 24 hours away, getting pre-approved, and submitting documents. If they're serious, they should have no problem following the processes you have established in your business.

The next one, which is a controversial one, because I know a lot of agents do this a differently, but part of my process is that a buyer must sign a buyer's representation agreement. This is only if we're going to be working together. Before I go out showing someone a home, or even if it's passing them off to one my vendors, we're going to establish that we will be working together. If someone is not willing to sign your buyer's representation contract, then they're probably not a serious buyer. They may just want to extract information from you or get contacts from you. These fake buyers just want you take them out and show them a ton of properties, and they don't want to do what's required to give you the confidence that you'll get paid. Ask yourself, why would anyone have a problem with signing something that protects both parties? They're getting the result that they want, and you're getting what you need to make it happen.

It's all part of the process. The representation agreement argument comes up a lot. Beware, people who don't sign for you to be their agent, especially after you put in work with them, are most likely going to be that client that uses you for your time and resources and turns around only to work with another agent. Sometimes, they go and call their family member who has their real estate license to get them to do all the contracts and get paid from the transaction. You don't want to spin your wheels trying to work with someone who doesn't want to be loyal to you. You want to always make your working agreements are mutual. It's not fair for us as the agents to do all the work with a buyer, not willing to cooperate, and so why do it?

The last type of fake buyer is kind of a no brainer. They are those buyers who don't communicate. Before I get too far ahead, I understand everybody's busy. I'm busy. You're busy. We're all busy, but there's a level of communication that needs to happen when someone is buying a home. These fake buyers extract information from you, and then they disappear for some reason or another. You try to reach them, but they're not answering your text messages, not answering your emails, and dodging your phone calls. Clearly, they're not a serious buyer.

I encourage you to reach out to them a few times, but if they're not returning any communication, then they're most likely not a serious buyer. In their heads, they've probably thinking *based on everything that this agent has put me through, this is getting really serious, and I better just disappear before I get myself too far into this*.

If someone disappears on me and goes ghost, luckily, I didn't invest a lot of time and money into that person who wasn't serious. If someone doesn't want to work with you, no hard feelings. There are tons of buyers out there, and you can easily spot the ones who are actually serious from the ones who aren't serious, simply through those actions.

The serious buyers are the ones that you want to focus your time and energies on because they're going to really appreciate it, and you're going to make money from working with them. For the ones that aren't that serious, you can keep them in your database, put them on your drip campaign, do whatever to stay in front of them, but don't go out showing a ton of properties when they don't want to even get pre-approved, they don't want to discuss finances, they don't want to sign a buyer's rep with you, and they don't want to communicate with you. Especially, when you try and try to communicate with them. It's just not worth your time. You'll notice these things. There's a better way to run your business.

Perfect your process and know what you're worth. Don't waste time on the tire kickers.

Part Six
Working The Business

First 2 Weeks On The Job

I literally remember the exact moment that I got my real estate license and how excited I felt. I felt like I was on top of the world. The first few days as a Realtor, you're literally running around like a chicken with its head cut off. Theres so many possibility and theres so much you want to accomplish. It can be quite the rush.

As I recall my first few weeks as a Realtor in this chapter, I'll be laying out a few expectations, so that you can know what you're destined to experience. I'm not going to give you every single tiny thing you will experience, that can be a whole book in itself. I am however, going to fill you in on a few common things most new real estate agents experience in the first 14 days of becoming and active and licensed real estate agent.

Let's go ahead and get right into it.

The first thing you can expect is to feel extremely overwhelmed. Let me tell you, this is completely normal and pretty much every new agent experiences it. After you've worked really hard to get your license, you're ready to work. You want to get it done immediately. The time you will begin to feel most overwhelmed will be when you realize, you don't know exactly what to do. There's so many things coming at you from so many different directions, but let me restate this; it is perfectly normal, so don't freak out. Take it one day at a time and focus your energy on one task at a time.

The second thing you can expect, and a lot of people aren't going to like this, but you expect to come out with some more money after you get licensed. When you become officially licensed, you are now a business owner and what do business owners have to do? They have to invest in their businesses. You're going to have to make some personal and business investments. A few things you're going to have to pay for are association fees, brokerage fees, business cards, lockboxes, and business phone numbers just to name a few. All of these are out of pocket expenses. Here's my advice on this: Only pay for what you absolutely need for the moment. Just the necessities.

Another thing you can expect is for your phone number and your email to be flooded with advertisements and solicitations. As a new business, many people are going to try to sell you something that they feel can help your business. Here's my advice on that. If it sounds too good to be true, it most likely is. Think smart and use your best judgment when it comes to things like this. I have a chapter devoted to advice on buying Internet leads and the types of companies that are going to be calling you. It will really open your eyes up to the tricks.

The last thing you can expect in your first two weeks as a Realtor is to not close a deal. I'm not trying to be negative or anything, I'm all about the positivity, but I also believe in being realistic. Just because you've become a Realtor, doesn't mean deals are just going to start falling from thin air. You will have to work and network and then work and work, but don't worry. If you put in the work, business is going to come. It just may not come in the first two weeks.

It Starts With One Client

My first tip to help you land your first real estate client and eventually have your first deal is to inform your network that you're a licensed real estate agent. This is very important. This includes friends, family, coworkers at your job, or your church. Anybody and everybody. Let the world know that you are now a real estate agent, and that you're essentially looking for business. You don't want to become a secret agent because if you're a secret agent, nobody's going to know that you're in real estate, and nobody's going to send you business. It's very important that you let everybody know that you are now a real estate agent. Not only are you an agent, but you have passed your test. Hopefully, you are with a great brokerage, and you have some awesome people behind you, and you're ready to get to work.

Tip number two is to immediately start hosting open houses. As a new agent, I realize that you may not have any listings, and you may not even know how to get listings, so the best thing you can do is volunteer to host an open house for another agent. In most real estate offices, there are agents that will have listings and may not have a lot of time to hold them open. I would simply compose an email directly to the agent who has some listings and kindly ask them, *"Do you mind if I hold your home or your listing open this weekend?:* The good thing about this is that the other agent is representing the listing, and you can represent any buyers that come through the door. Any buyers that walk into your open house, are leads for you, and they can eventually turn into your first client. This is one of the best ways that you can get in front of people who are interested in real estate. They are easy targets because they're coming into an open house. Use your scripts, talk to them, and let your personality shine.

When speaking to open house visitors, start to build rapport with them. These are people who you most likely don't know, so they're going to be the people who can really get your database and pipeline building. I don't want to lead you on, so I'm not saying that they're going to immediately start working with you. You've still got to keep your real estate hat on, and you need to follow up, follow up, follow up. That's the name of this game. You really have to follow up with them, but these are people whom you've had a warm introduction to. They're not just random off the internet. They've literally walked into a door of a home where you are, and you've most likely had the opportunity to be there with them for 5 to 10 minutes, maybe even longer. That's your opportunity to really establish that relationship. Even if they're just looking, which everybody says, *"We're just looking,"* they've obviously walked in there for a reason. They may be looking for themselves right now or maybe for themselves in the future. They could be looking for a family member. They could simply be a neighbor. Neighbors are my favorite because they want to see how the home is presented. You may want to talk to them about listing their home. There are so many hidden opportunities. You've just got to take advantage of them.

My third tip is to host a first-time home buyer seminar. There are people in your city that are currently searching for information that we as real estate agents have. You should partner with a loan officer, an escrow attorney, or a title company to host the first-time home buyer seminar. Doing this can yield some great results. I've done these in the past, and I'll normally have around 20 to 30 people who come in and just want information on how to buy a home. It doesn't have to cost you a lot of money. You don't have to make it extravagant or anything. Choose a day of the week, and for one or two hours, explain what the process is like to purchase a home. You don't have to go into great detail. As a matter of fact, you want to keep it more surface level, so that people can understand it. If you partner with a loan officer or a closing attorney, he or she can back you up to answer those questions you may not know.

Seminars are a great way for you to get clients and get your name and brand out there. Just spending two hours of your time explaining your process can allow you to walk out with multiple clients. Just be the professional that you are and rock the crap out of that first-time home buyer seminar.

Next, start to practice cold calling. This involves picking up the phone and calling people that you may not know. There are two categories of people that I normally call. The first category is for sale by owners. You'll often see those labeled as FSBOs. FSBO's are people who have their home on the market, and they're trying to sell their homes themselves without an agent. Alongside FSBOs, we call homeowners who have expired listings. An expired listing is a home that has been on the market with another agent, but they weren't able to sell it. Now they are called expired listings. These two are going to be your easiest cold calls to do because they have already expressed the willingness to sell. When calling them, you want to have your scripts ready and memorized as much as possible. Your mission is to get across to them that you're the right agent for the job of getting their home sold.

Last but not least, you should get comfortable asking for referrals. Simply asking someone for a referral can go a long way. If you are a part of any networking groups, if you go to any sporting events, or if you run any organizations; those are the perfect people to ask for business. This is one thing that most agents don't do. They don't ask people for the business. If I call you, and you tell me you're not looking right now, or you don't want to buy a home right now, that's okay; my next question to you would be, *"Who do you know that does want to purchase a home?"* or *"Who do you know that may be looking for an apartment or somewhere to rent?"* It's important that you maximize the opportunities when you are communicating. Therefore, you've got to ask people for business. If you don't ask them, you're never going to get it. It's scary to think about but someone else is going to get that business because he or she simply asked the right question.

Best Ways To Get Your First

I'm sure I've made it pretty how it can be so confusing during your first few months when you don't know exactly what to do. I didn't know who to call, what to talk about, or even what to say. I just played the game of trial and error and tried different things. Luckily, being in the business for a while, I have found that there are some surefire ways that pretty much anybody can use to get clients into their real estate business. This is not a secret formula. As a matter of fact, there is no secret formula to make you a top-producing real estate agent, but there are strategies, and there are processes that you can use that will get you clientele. These ways will get you going and put you in the positions where you can market and sell to people. Those are the strategies that I want to discuss.

There are two main places that I recommend to anybody who's new in the business or wants to ramp up the amount of leads they have coming in. The first one, and this may seem like an obvious one, is your personal database. When I mention personal database, I'm not talking about a CRM system or anything like that; I'm literally talking about your network.

It's the people you know.

Everyone has a database of people. Whether it's just the contacts in your phone, or everyone you know on social media, you have a database. If you have friends, family, and coworkers, those people are going to be your starting points of contact. They are going to be the easiest people that you can potentially get a deal from. Your personal contacts are already people who know, like, and trust you. They should want to help you succeed.

There's a special way to actually go about doing that. I really wrapped my head around this whole concept of the personal database based off the book, <u>The Power of Who</u>, by Bob Beaudine. It's a great read, and you should read it after you read this one. On the book cover it says, *"You already know everyone you need to know,"* and that's so true. If you think about it, you already know everyone who you need to know to reach any person you need to reach. We are all connected in some way. For instance, many people are connected to me through my YouTube channel. Personally, I know a lot of people through my business associations and my personal network. A lot of the business owners I know are very well connected. I know someone who could probably help you do just about anything. If they can't then they know someone who can. Then the person they refer you to probably knows someone who can maybe even contribute to your efforts. It keeps going on and on. You could literally reach the President of the United States just through the people that you already know and the people that they know. When you really start to use your personal database of people to its maximum potential, you'll be surprised what can happen.

A simple exercise you can do is just pick up your phone, open your phone book, and start to call people and let them know that you're in real estate. See if they know anyone who could potentially want to do something when it comes to real estate. Whether it's buying, selling, or leasing, you want that persons information. I promise you that if you do this, you're going to get at least one referral.

The same concept applies to social media. Instead of just making social media posts about your being in real estate, actually go through the process of messaging people and asking them for business or referrals. You'd be surprised what can happen from that.

The problem that I see with a lot of people, especially when it comes to the database, is that they are afraid to ask. They use excuses like, "*I don't know what to say*." Which is simply just a pride thing. Others have those thoughts in their heads telling them, "*That person doesn't know anyone* or *I know they don't want to do anything in real estate,*" before they even ask. You're already discounting your contacts without solid evidence. Remember, it's not necessarily about whether they want to do something with real estate or not, it's about whom they know that possibly wants to do something concerning real estate. Don't discount your phone book because you think that somebody is not going to want to buy or sell a house. Today, people know a lot of people, and you'd be surprised whom you can get in contact with by simply asking that question.

Next, we'll discuss social media marketing. We all know social media is the present and the future. Everyone, it seems like, is on social media. The only person I know who's not on social media is my little brother. It's so surprising that he doesn't have a Facebook or an Instagram or anything like that, but everyone else I know is on social media including my grandmother. When I talk about social media marketing in this instance, I'm not talking about creating posts, graphics, or videos. I'm talking about reaching out to people, letting them know what you do and asking for their help.

Something that a lot of us don't practice is vulnerability. Being vulnerable enough to ask for help is uncomfortable for real estate agents. If you simply reach out to somebody and say, *"I'm looking to build my business. It's been really tough out here. Can you help me?"* you're going to get a totally different response than if you just message a run-on sentence to someone saying, *"I'm a real estate agent who can help you with all of your buying and selling needs, so if you happen to know anybody who wants to do anything with real estate, here's my number, my website, and my email address. You can contact me here anytime."* Many agents do that, and they wonder why they don't get responses or get blocked and unfriended. If you genuinely approach someone as a true person and ask for help, you're going get a totally different response and possibly some business.

Here's a little Facebook algorithm secret. As you start to message people, your profile will begin to show up more in their newsfeed and timelines. When that starts to happen, you can then begin to publish those marketing pieces out there constantly reminding people what you do. Staying in the forefront of someone's mind can go a long way. This was something that I did when I really got going in the business. I made sure anybody and everybody knew that I sold real estate, and that was how I was able to really get my leads flowing in. The secret was simply asking for help by reaching out to people. All of those different tactics, in addition to all the cold calling, postcards, and mailing letters made the biggest difference.

Think for a moment how many friends you may have on your social media networks combined. I want you to add them all up: Facebook, Instagram, Twitter, Snapchat, and any others out there. Out of all the people you have counted, do you think you could get at least 1 referral out of them?

Traps With Buying Leads

The first thing when it comes to buying leads, whether they're from a website or someone just randomly called you on the phone promising to bring you some business, is that you want to make sure that you are a closer. If you're wondering what a closer is, it's someone who can actually make the sale or solidify the business opportunity. Before you jump to the conclusion that all online lead sources suck, just know, you've still got to be a real estate agent, and you have to know how to close people over the phone.

In your career, you're more than likely going to have an internet lead show up in your inbox, and you need to know how to be a top salesperson to convert those leads over to clients of yours. Something that I see a lot of agents do is— get a lead call or an email that someone has filled out from the website, so they'll call them. The people will say, *"Oh, we're already working with the agent,"* or *"No, we don't need your help."*

The agent will just hang up the phone after saying *"Okay, thank you."*

What???

That's not being a closer.

You need to know how to ask the right questions and convert them over to at least having a meeting with you. You'll want to quickly ask, *"Well, what initially brought you to the website?"* If they say they're not looking, you can also ask *"Since you're not looking to purchase a home, were you looking for somebody else?"* It's your job to uncover what they are really doing. To do this, simply ask the right questions to discover what their true motives behind their actions are. Once you master how to do that, half the battle is done.

Your true missions is to get new people in front of you as quickly as possible, but it's not as easy as you think it may be. If you feel unprepared, you consider investing in a skills training course or practice some scrips with different closing techniques. Invest your time into something that will help turn you into a closer.

I'm going to let you know that when it comes to actually paying for leads and buying leads, it can be quite expensive, especially if you don't know what you're doing. Most of the lead services that are available are going to start at a minimum of $250 a month, and they'll go up from there.

Here's how the lead service providers commonly work. There's a lot of the websites out there, and I'm not going to name any names, but a lot of the popular real estate websites out there sell leads to Realtors. What they do is either charge you per impression or by click (contact). An impression means, every time your information shows up on a webpage, you get charged for it. The charges are put into a package, just to make it easy. They sell you a package that is going to guarantee your face or your profile is seen a certain number of times. They may charge $250 or $300 for 1000 impressions.

That means you're going to get charged $250 for 1000 times of your face being shown. Don't be fooled by this high number of impressions. This doesn't guarantee that the people are going to click on your face or that you're going to get that lead, it's simply just the amount being charged to you.

When the lead services charge you per click, it's going to cost you every time a visitor clicks on your profile. In this instance, they try to sell you a package where they guarantee a certain number of clicks to your profile. I prefer paying for leads this way versus the impressions because at least I know that people are clicking on my profile or possibly even clicking onto my website. If I get a good number of clicks to my website but no contacts, it's probably something on my website that I need to fix to make the conversions increase.

When you begin working with a real estate leads website, the costs will vary by the location of your leads. A lot of these services charge per zip code. Certain zip codes are ranked more valuable than other zip codes. What I've learned in my experiences with choosing a zip code is not to necessarily go for the zip code with the most expensive homes. I've tried it, and I have found that clients looking in the multi-million-dollar property price range and up, are not looking on these websites to find their next agent.

Before you choose the zip code, do some research on your markets. Open your MLS and really do some research. Look and find what zip codes people are buying the most homes in. It could be at a price point of $150,000 or $200,000. These price points are very affordable for many people so there is probably more activity in these areas. The buyers shopping in those price points are more of the buyers that are looking on these real estate websites for homes. Starting out, it'll probably be a lot more effective for you, if you choose a lower priced point zip code just to build up your sales and credibility.

Also, be sure to take a look at which zip codes have the most listings and take note of how many transactions are being closed on average in that zip code. See how often they're being closed, meaning the average days on market. That's the information that you need to know so that you can really make an informed decision when it comes to purchasing a zip code from one of these lead services.

I always like to tell agents that most of the services out there are going to put you into a contract because they want to guarantee your money for at least six months to a year. Just be prepared to put that money up if you choose to subscribe to a lead service. They can't guarantee that you will close any business but they can guarantee that you will pay them.

I believe that there are so many ways to generate leads, organically, including cold calling, social media, and networking, but if you choose to go down the route where you're going to pay a website to generate leads for you, make sure that you ask the right questions. Here are some questions that you should ask, aside from whether you pay per impression or click.

Are you going to be the only agent featured on the listings in that zip code?

How many other agents are featured on the same page?

Is there any type of guarantee on the lead quality?

Some websites out there put you up against maybe three or four other agents, and the client just pretty much picks which agents they want to contact them. It's kinda like a dating app where the person swipes left or right based on just a name and a picture. I would just be cautious on spending a ton of money on this. Remember, when you speak to the companies, they are salespeople. They will make it sound very tempting. I recommend starting low and then increasing your advertisement spending as you begin to see results.

I purchased the wrong leads after I had my first closing because I didn't know what I was doing. Not only did I not know which leads to purchase, but I didn't know how to be a closer yet. I didn't choose the right zip codes. I didn't do any of the things that I'm telling you now. That's why it just turned out to be a big waste of money for me.

To sum it all up, be sure to ask the right questions, make sure you have some closing techniques ready, make sure that you answer your phone when leads call, and most importantly, make sure that you can afford it. None of these sources are going to turn you into a super-agent or make you rich. I believe that they just need to be a supplement to what you're already doing and add to the places you're already organically getting leads from.

Good Investments To Make

The first really good investment for real estate agents to make it is to invest in a good CRM for your business. What is a CRM? CRM stands for Customer Relationship Management, and it is basically something that you're going to use to place all of your leads, your contacts, and your transactions in. You're going to need some type of software that will allow you to do this. There are so many different CRM options in the marketplace that you can use to manage your real estate business. A really good CRM can be an investment, so plan to invest in a good one from the start. Doing this at the start of your career will save you so many headaches along the way.

Think of it like an asset to you, especially with keeping your business organized. You will be able to closely and easily manage your leads, clients, and your business. With a good CRM, you will keep good contact records and know exactly when and how often you have followed up with leads.

Secondly, you're going to want to get the word out about your business and what better way these days than social media? Consider investing in some well written and attractive, professional Facebook and Instagram ads. I run ads all the time in my business. They let me capture new audiences and get in front of people that I don't personally know. Ads are a good way to start getting your name out there to help you start generating leads. Get familiar with how to run Facebook and Instagram ads or plan to hire somebody to do it for you. It is a good investment, which you're going to really want to get going in your business early on.

Since we're talking about ads, you'll want to be sure you have a good website, so invest in a professional website for your real estate business. Your website needs to be resourceful and filled with information. Be sure to include some type of property search. Imagine what a new lead or a new client would want to see when they go to your website. On my website I have lots of information about me, my team, buyer resources, and seller resources. A good website can do half the work for you. It doesn't have to be too expensive. Although, out of all my investment recommendations, this is going to be the one that may cost you the most money. The good thing is that once it's established, you really don't have to touch it too much more after that.

Last but not least, you want to invest in a good coaching program. I believe we all need coaches at various levels within the business. Coaches can help bring your dreams to reality. You want someone to guide you from point A to B. I would recommend getting involved in a great coaching program or seeking out a personal coach or mentor. This is going to cost you a little money because you are paying for someone else's time. It's not going to be the most expensive thing you invest in, but it's going to be the most valuable. A coach can be the one thing to attribute to you and your success in the real estate business. Through coaching programs, we get roadmaps, instructions, accountability, and direction. With direction, you receive clarity. It's always great to follow someone who's already been where you are trying to go.

Bad Investments To Make

We've talked about good investments, and now it's time to recognize the spending of money in unnecessary places. I've done so much of that, so I feel like I can speak about this topic very well. I'm going to tell you a few things that you can watch out for so that you don't make the same mistakes that I did and unnecessarily waste money.

The first thing that you want to steer away from in order to avoid spending unnecessary money is overdoing open houses. You probably watched some of the real estate

TV shows and have seen some of the extravagant open house parties that they host. They have servers, live music, bartenders, and expensive cars, which is cool, but not always necessary. Going all out and creating a production of an open house should solely depend on the value of the property. There's no need to have a catering company serve food for every open house you do. Depending on the price point, it's appropriate and common to have cookies, something to drink, or other light bites for people to snack on if they want to. Don't feel like you must have your open houses catered by Gordon Ramsay. You will be hosting open houses too frequently to invest a lot of money into each one.

In a previous chapter I mentioned all of the sales calls you'll receive. Once word gets out that you're a Realtor, your phone is going to blow up with people who are trying to sell you stuff. People love to sell advertising. It's so easy because we feel like we always need another way to advertise. People will tell you *"You can be at the top of the search engines if you'll just pay us a small monthly fee."* There are so many of these solicitors out there. I'm telling you now, don't spend your money on them. I'm not saying that they don't work, but it's one of those things that you can do yourself if you take the time to learn how.

Surprisingly, doing your own advertising is not that hard. Once you begin to pay a company to do it, you're going to have to keep paying them, over and over and over again because they're not doing something that's going to provide you with organic, lasting results. It's one of those things that, as long as you're paying for it, then you'll get the results, but once you stop paying them, you're pretty much off the search engines. When you get into search engine marketing and ranking, you really want organic search engine results. Organic results last, and they're free.

I've paid for ads in some crazy places, and they just never gave me that return that I was looking for. It can be a magazine, a newspaper, a shopping cart at the grocery store, or even sponsoring some football fields. These things are great for exposure and name recognition, but you just never get the return on investment that you think that you're going to get. Steer away from spending excessive money on sponsorships and ads. Realize, most people just throw that stuff away, or they may look at it one time and that's it.

Another thing that is a waste of money is spending money on expensive business cards. Now, I know you're going to be super excited as a Realtor, and you're to going want really nice business cards, but there is no need to spend lot of money on business cards. Most of the time, people throw them away, and to be honest with you, I don't really even carry around business cards a lot. I'll keep a couple on me, but if somebody needs my contact information, I'm going to try to put their information in my phone, so I can get their information and reach out to them in the future. If I give somebody my business card, there's no guarantee that they're going to contact me, so I would rather be the one in control.

Part 6
Working The Business

Customer Relationship Management

As we are talking about investments, my goal in this chapter is to help you choose the right CRM for your real estate business. How I'm going to do that is by telling you what specific features to look for when choosing one. Before I tell you the features and functions to look out for when you're choosing a CRM, let's recap what a CRM is. The letters C, R, and M stand for customer relationship management, and it's essentially a tool that you can use to manage your customers and manage your clients. CRM's are widely used in a variety of industries, but we see them most commonly used in sales professions.

When you are choosing a CRM for your real estate business, the first thing that you want to look for is a CRM that has an easy setup process. We're busy in real estate, and we want to work. We want to get to closing deals, so it's not the best use of our time to sit and build a CRM or try to figure out how to use it. You want something that's going to have an easy setup. You want something that you'll be able to log into, and it's ready to go for you. Now, of course, it's not going to have all of your customer information in it, but you want it built specifically for your real estate business, so that way it's not so hard to get started using it.

Next, you want to ask the question when choosing a CRM. Can it support your full sales pipeline? I know that sounds a bit complicated, so let me break that down. Your full sales pipeline is the act of getting someone in as a lead to getting them to the closing table. You want something that can support every single step of your actual process. It needs to keep track of where your leads are coming from and what's happening with each one specifically. You want something that gives you options to place leads into different categories, so that you can reach out to people at the right times and for the right reasons.

Next you want to make sure that it can support your customer life cycle. What that simply means is when someone comes in as a lead and has turned it into a client, just because you've sold their home does not mean that they should be deleted or that they are out of sight and out of mind. You want something that can manage someone from a lead to a new client, to a past client, then to a repeat client. Just the full life cycle. When I work with people, I like to be their Realtor for life, so I need a CRM that can manage that and that can give me those capabilities in it.

My final question to help you decide on a CRM is can you access it on the go? Mobility is so important. You want something that you can take from place to place and isn't going to just hold you in front of a computer. I've worked with CRM's in the past where they didn't really have a mobile version, or they at least didn't have a good mobile version. I felt like I could only update it or access it when I was sitting in front of my computer. You want something that's going to do a lot better than that. If it has a mobile app or, at least, a mobile-friendly website, then that is just as useful as being behind the computer and will set you up in a much better position to use it while you're on the go.

Cold Calling Strategy

If you remember from earlier in the book, I told you I actually got my first listing through cold calling, so now it's very appropriate that give you a few of my cold calling techniques, so that it'll hopefully help you as you try to get business. These are things that have worked for me, and I think that they'll work for you, too.

When you first begin cold calling, the best thing and the first step that you need to do is find some scripts. You need to find a script that perhaps others have used or had success with. There are so many scripts out on different websites, including my own so they shouldn't be hard to come by. You simply need to find the right scripts that work for you and match your style.

Once you get those scripts, the next thing you need to do is internalize them. Basically, you want to practice them...a lot You want to get familiar with how scripts work, and you want to get comfortable reading them. You don't want to get on the phone and sound like you're actually reading from a script. People can tell. Really letting those scripts become part of your language through memorization will really help. Most real estate scripts are pretty similar, so once you get the gist of them and know the ways people tend to respond, you can know how to respond back to them. It gets a lot easier, but you're only going to get better if you start reading them and really memorizing them.

Next, you want to practice. I recommend that you get in front of a mirror or maybe find a buddy who's in real estate with you and practice cold calling. Wake up in the morning 30 minutes earlier just go over the scripts. Make it a habit to go over maybe two or three scripts a day and just practice, practice, practice. When you do this, you will get comfortable talking. You will get comfortable with how your voice sounds, and your partner can give you valuable and constructive feedback. They will really know how you actually sound on the other line.

The next thing you want to do is get a list of contacts. Now that you have the scripts and you've memorized and practiced them, you need people to call. I recommend subscribing to a service or manually creating a list of expired listings or for sale by owners through the information you find online.

You can use a website like whitepages.com, and these will give you phone numbers of people that have their phone numbers registered. There are lots of services online that can research names and numbers of people who have expired in your local MLS or the for sale by owners in your local market. They will give you those addresses and phone numbers.

You're going to need a list because you're going to need people to actually cold call. When you're calling people, I recommend that you stand up. It gives you a better sound. It gets your blood flowing and gives you better energy while you're making calls. I know a lot of agents, including myself, that'll put their scripts on the wall, so they can look at them easily, so I recommend doing that.

Place them at eye-level standing up because it makes a difference when you're actually making the cold calls and using the scripts.

Lastly, you've just got to do it. Cold calling is a bit intimidating, and it is a little scary. It was scary for me when I first started doing it, but you'll only get better at it as you practice more by actually doing it. You'll want to get on the phone with some live homeowners, some potential buyers, some sellers, etc. Get on the phone with them, and you'll start to notice similarities. You'll see that they pretty much all, for the most part, say the same things. As time goes on, those scripts will just start coming out naturally, and you won't even need them on your wall anymore. Try those things and I hope they help.

Final Tips For New Agents

"This is a career. Real estate is a career. You build it, and you can make a lot of money if you treat it like one. "

- Me

My first tip for new agents is get really good at figuring things out for yourself. If you've always been one of those people who've always had your hand held and someone telling you step-by-step what to do by giving you direction, realize real estate isn't anything like that. You need to get good at figuring things out for yourself. There's a lot to be learned. There's a lot of things you will want to learn. As agents, we always feel we need to know exactly what to do and say. The trick is to use the internet to get your questions answered. Google is so powerful. By using the Internet, you can get really good at figuring things out.

There's not always going to be somebody there to hold your hand and give you step-by-step instructions on what to do. You've got to be an adult in this career and in this industry. You've got to learn how to research and take instruction. Remember, most agents are your competition. They don't necessarily want to help you because they feel like you will take business away from them.

My second tip is you need to be vulnerable, especially if you're a new agent. You don't know a lot. You're walking into a career, and you're really trying to figure it out and make your mark in the industry. To do this, you need to be vulnerable. I'm mostly talking about being vulnerable with your clients. You don't need to walk into every client's home or speak with every client pretending to know everything and know how to do everything. If there's something that you don't know, tell them! You can say, *"I don't know that, but I will get you the answer."* Just be honest with people. If you even want to go as far as saying, *"This is my first transaction. I have a great team behind me. I had people helping me all along the way, and I appreciate you for giving me this opportunity."* That can go so much further than trying to show and act like you're the biggest, baddest agency in the city.

Also, be vulnerable with your learning. This goes down to your brokerage. Ask questions when appropriate. Talk to people about certain situations that you're having. You're not an expert. There are not many people who are experts in this industry. It's forever changing, and you need to really learn how to be vulnerable because that's when things are going to open up for you. People are going to want to help you out and help you to succeed.

My third tip, and this one makes a lot of people uncomfortable, is to be prepared to put yourself out there. This is one of those careers in which it's all about your image, and it is all about your knowledge. It's your business and you've got to be prepared to put yourself out there. Whether we're talking about images, blogs, writings, social media, videos, etc. You've got to put yourself in the public eye. That's what's going to attract people to you and make them want to work with you as their agent.

When you start putting yourself out there publicly and providing value through showing that you are knowledgeable and have a great image, it's going to attract people to you. No one is going to know about you if you want to play the role of a secret agent.

If you're just behind the desk, behind the office wall, nobody really knows about you. What's going to make your phone ring? What's going to make someone want to reach out to you? You must be prepared. If you really want to make a mark in this industry and really be successful, you've got to put yourself out there. Social media is everything, so as a real estate agent, you must jump on that. I mean, I understand if you're shy or you're not really comfortable with it, but my advice is still to get comfortable with it because it's not going anywhere. Long gone are the days when people opened up a phone book to look for a real estate agent's name and number. Today, it's all about the internet. It's all about who has the biggest message out there and networking.

My next tip is to attend as many training classes as possible. Even when you get your license, it doesn't stop there. All throughout your real estate career, you're going to want to get trained. Different things are going to come up. Things change in the industry. New tools, new tips, and new processes. are very common, so attending as many training classes as possible can help.

So many people offer training in this industry. I get emails all day and night from title companies, mortgage companies, attorneys, banks, everyone offering some type of training class to help us in our businesses. Even as a seasoned agent, we all attend trainings. There's always something to learn. The more knowledge you have, the more power you have, so attend as much training as you can.

My next tip is to treat your real estate business like a job. Hold yourself accountable. If you're transitioning from a part-time or full-time job into real estate, there's going to be a lot of changes. There's not going to be a boss waking you up in the morning. There's not going to be a clock in, clock out. You're not going to receive a paycheck every two weeks or every month or weekly. It's totally different. You're working for yourself. You set your own hours. You go at your own pace. You do what you want to do. You need to be very disciplined and treat this like a job.

Surround yourself with people who are disciplined in their real estate businesses. I always tell people winning is a culture, and you want to be around winners. Winners are the ones who wake up early and the ones who work, work, work, grind, grind, grind, and treat this like a true business.

The sixth tip is to learn to take direction. What that's going to require is for you to get good at listening.

Don't try to reinvent the wheel in this business. If you have a mentor, or if you're part of my coaching program, listen to what your coach or your mentor is telling you. Oftentimes, I see people who get into the real estate business, and they want to try to do things their way and then figure out why it's not working. If you're joining the brokerage, and they have an extensive training program, there's a good chance that someone or many people have done all of those things and they actually work! If you want to succeed in this business, learn from people who are successful and follow their programs.

My next tip, and this is something that I struggled with in the beginning of my business, is that you need to be okay with being uncomfortable. There are going to be so many situations in which you are going to be very uncomfortable, and it's going to require you to step outside of your comfort zone. I wasn't an expert at door knocking. I wasn't an expert at cold calling. Honestly, I was terrified of it. I couldn't imagine picking up the phone, calling a random person, trying to get a listing. I couldn't even imagine walking up to someone at a network or event and striking up a conversation. All of those things were so uncomfortable for me, but I said to myself that I had to stop being that way because I'm never going to be able to progress as long as I am comfortable. I was letting that fear hold me back. Be okay with being uncomfortable. Just know that there is a light at the end of the tunnel, and it won't be this way for long.

Next, don't look for instant gratification. This business takes a while. There is a ramp up period. There is an amount of time that it's going to take for you to get your name out there and for your phone to start ringing. Don't think just because you've posted something on Facebook in the morning that your phone is going to be ringing by the evening. Don't think because you met someone at a bar that they're going to call you to be their Realtor. This stuff takes time. It's going to require you to work very hard, long hours, sleepless nights, but eventually, it will pay off. You must stay very persistent in your actions. Just because something didn't work the first time, the second time, the fifth time, does not mean that you should give up. It's actually a statistic in cold calling, that it can take at least eight follow-ups before someone will even give you the attention that you're looking for. Being a real estate agent is not a business of instant gratification, and if that's what you want, I would say find another career because unless you've already made a big name for yourself and can just hop into selling, you're most likely not going to sell something for a little while. You need to be okay with that. I know that most real estate agents had to go through this journey. They had to take time to put themselves out there to develop a name for themselves. I didn't become who I am overnight. Once you start to look at it that way, it makes life a lot easier and it'll save you on frustrations as you are building your real estate business. Your efforts will payoff.

Next, you need to budget and save your money appropriately. If you have a job, whether it's a full-time or part-time job, and you're just getting started, keep your job, unless you have money saved up. You'll get to a point that you can leave your other job and work real estate full time, but if you don't have that cushion, don't quit your job. You need to budget appropriately. You need to save money. You're going to spend a lot of money in this career, especially once you start getting listings, entertaining clients, and taking buyers out. Hosting an event will cost you money, so if you don't have that nest egg, you need to keep doing whatever you're doing to make money right now and slowly transition over. It's okay, not everybody can hop into real estate full-time. I don't want you sleeping on the street or homeless trying to build your real estate career. Just be smart about your financial choices when it comes to this.

My last tip is that you need to always be on alert. You are a brand. You are going to build a name for yourself as you become successful. You need to be on alert when you're out in the public eye. Always know that there are people watching, and you're in the business of satisfying other people. You're trying to gain business, and you're going to want to get clients. Don't let your name be tarnished by letting foolish pictures or headlines get out there. You don't want that. I'm so careful about this because you never know who's watching or who's listening. The higher you get; the more people will try to break you down. This is a fact, from my personal experiences. Not everyone is for your success. Real estate has its positives, but we can't ignore the haters, backstabbers, cheaters, and scammers.

You can also be on alert in a positive way. If you're in a restaurant, and you hear someone talking about real estate at the next table over, be friendly and talk to them, maybe even strike up a conversation. You can let them know that you're the expert in the area and offer some real estate advice. Don't hard sell people, but always be on alert, the bad and the good.

As you embark on this journey, I want you to remember everything you have read so far in this book.

Although we are all different, at the end of the day, we are all human. We get uncomfortable, we get shy, we get happy, and we get sad. It's just natural. How you perform as a real estate agent is solely based on how you control your actions and your feelings. You are the only ultimately in control of what happens from this point forward. No one, and I mean no one is going to make you the next big real estate agent so realize it's all on you.

Best of luck to you and thanks for reading.
- Chastin

About The Author

Chastin J. Miles is a full-service real estate agent specializing in Dallas real estate, brand management, and client representation in a comprehensive spectrum of classes including single-family residential, condos and developments, commercial real estate, and luxury leases.

Miles and his team aim to bring a new perspective to the traditional real estate transaction by extending far beyond the offerings of conventional agents. Chastin J. Miles strives to be both a lifestyle agent committed to informing and connecting our local communities, and an agent offering design, marketing, and sales solutions for buyers, sellers, developers, and local and international investors.

Miles' work background, education, and passion have helped him to become a top producing real estate agent. Miles is an agent who understands that buying a home is one of the largest purchases a client will make. His mission is to provide each client with the best sales and marketing tools to get their property sold, while providing an open line of communication to keep his clients engaged in each step of the process. One of Miles' top priorities is to produce the highest return for his client's investment.

As a native Texan, Miles is no stranger to the competitive Texas real estate market. His background in sales, marketing, and brand management has given him a foundation for success in all aspects of the home buying and selling process. Whether it is implementing a strong marketing campaign or negotiating a contract, Miles strives to produce the best results for his clients. His enthusiastic attitude and strong work ethic make him one of North Texas' top agents.

In addition to working with clients, Miles serves as the Social Media chairperson for the MetroTex Young Professionals Network, hosts the Millennial Movers Series podcast on iTunes, and was recently awarded the prestigious Healy Hustle Award. He was also named "Mr. Branding" by his peers for his unique and effective approach to marketing in the competitive home market. He has been featured in numerous publications including The Dallas Morning News, CEO World Magazine, The Dallas Voice, BE GREAT Magazine, and more. You can also find many of Miles' writings on Inman News where he serves as a contributor in the real estate, social media, and marketing categories.

Chastin J. Miles published his first book, More Than Four Walls: The Ultimate Guide to Buying or Selling a Home in Dallas in 2016. This book empowers buyers and sellers with the knowledge and tools needed to navigate through today's competitive real estate marketplace. Buying and selling homes differs throughout the country, and this book is a go-to guide to flourish in the strong Dallas real estate market. Thousands rely on Miles' YouTube channel to gain insights on how to be successful in their own real estate careers and building their own brands.

Miles has made a way to give back to his peer community of real estate agents by launching the Industry Power Players Network. Inspired through his growing YouTube audience, Miles' mission is to empower, motivate, train, and educate the next generation of real estate agents and entrepreneurs through this network.

Miles' Real Estate team is constantly working to bring the best luxury real estate transaction. Miles and his team are experts at delivering smooth real estate transactions and have closed millions of dollars in real estate transactions to date.

For more information about the author, visit
www.chastinjmiles.com

Follow Chastin J. Miles on social media:
Facebook: facebook.com/ChastinJMilesOfficial
Twitter: twitter.com/chastinjmiles
LinkedIn: linkedin.com/in/chastinjmiles
YouTube: youtube.com/chastinjmiles
Instagram: instagram.com/chastinjmiles

Made in the USA
Middletown, DE
06 November 2021

51754812R00135